The Cambridge Book
of
Poetry for Children

PART I

CAMBRIDGE UNIVERSITY PRESS
C. F. CLAY, Manager
London: FETTER LANE, E.C.
Edinburgh: 100 PRINCES STREET

Bombay, Calcutta and Madras: MACMILLAN AND CO., Ltd.
Toronto: J. M. DENT AND SONS, Ltd.
Tokyo: THE MARUZEN-KABUSHIKI-KAISHA

Copyrighted in the United States of America by
G. P. PUTNAM'S SONS,
2, 4 AND 6, WEST 45TH STREET, NEW YORK CITY

The Cambridge Book

of

Poetry for Children

Edited by

KENNETH GRAHAME

Author of *The Golden Age, Dream Days, The Wind
in the Willows, etc.*

PART I

Cambridge :
at the University Press
1916

PREFACE

IN compiling a selection of Poetry for Children, a conscientious Editor is bound to find himself confronted with limitations so numerous as to be almost disheartening. For he has to remember that his task is, not to provide simple examples of the whole range of English poetry, but to set up a wicket-gate giving attractive admission to that wide domain, with its woodland glades, its pasture and arable, its walled and scented gardens here and there, and so to its sunlit, and sometimes misty, mountain-tops—all to be more fully explored later by those who are tempted on by the first glimpse. And always he must be proclaiming to the small tourists that there is joy, light and fresh air in that delectable country.

Briefly, I think that blank verse generally, and the drama as a whole, may very well be

left for readers of a riper age. Indeed, I
believe that those who can ignore the plays of
Shakespeare and his fellow-Elizabethans till
they are sixteen will be no losers in the long
run. The bulk, too, of seventeenth and
eighteenth century poetry, bending under its
burden of classical form and crowded classical
allusion, requires a completed education and
a wide range of reading for its proper
appreciation.

Much else also is barred. There are the
questions of subject, of archaic language and
thought, and of occasional expression, which
will occur to everyone. Then there is dialect,
and here one has to remember that these poems
are intended for use at the very time that a
child is painfully acquiring a normal—often
quite arbitrary—orthography. Is it fair to
that child to hammer into him—perhaps
literally—that porridge is spelt porridge, and
next minute to present it to him, in an official
'Reader,' under the guise of parritch? I think
not; and I have accordingly kept as far as
possible to the normal, though at some loss
of material.

In the output of those writers who have

deliberately written for children, it is surprising how largely the subject of *death* is found to bulk. Dead fathers and mothers, dead brothers and sisters, dead uncles and aunts, dead puppies and kittens, dead birds, dead flowers, dead dolls—a compiler of Obituary Verse for the delight of children could make a fine fat volume with little difficulty. I have turned off this mournful tap of tears as far as possible, preferring that children should read of the joy of life, rather than revel in sentimental thrills of imagined bereavement.

There exists, moreover, any quantity of verse for children, which is merely verse and nothing more. It lacks the vital spark of heavenly flame, and is useless to a selector of Poetry. And then there is the whole corpus of verse—most of it of the present day—which is written *about* children, and this has even more carefully to be avoided. When the time comes that we send our parents to school, it will prove very useful to the compilers of their primers.

All these restrictions have necessarily led to two results. First, that this collection is chiefly lyrical—and that, after all, is no bad thing. Lyric verse may not be representative of the whole range of English poetry, but as ‚an introduction to it, as a Wicket-gate, there is no better portal. The second result is, that it is but a small sheaf that these gleanings amount to; but for those children who frankly do not care for poetry it will be more than enough; and for those who love it and delight in it, no 'selection' could ever be sufficiently satisfying.

KENNETH GRAHAME.

October 1915.

CONTENTS

For Those a Little Older

Contents

For the Very Smallest Ones

RHYMES AND JINGLES

We begin with some jingles and old rhymes; for rhymes and jingles must not be despised. They have rhyme, rhythm, melody, and joy; and it is well for beginners to know that these are all elements of poetry, so that they will turn to it with pleasant expectation.

MERRY ARE THE BELLS

Merry are the bells, and merry would they
    ring,
Merry was myself, and merry could I sing;
With a merry ding-dong, happy, gay, and
    free,
And a merry sing-song, happy let us be!

Waddle goes your gait, and hollow are your
    hose;
Noddle goes your pate, and purple is your
    nose;
Merry is your sing-song, happy, gay, and
    free;
With a merry ding-dong, happy let us be!

Merry have we met, and merry have we been;
Merry let us part, and merry meet again;
With our merry sing-song, happy, gay, and free,
With a merry ding-dong, happy let us be!

SAFE IN BED

 Matthew, Mark, Luke and John,
 Bless the bed that I lie on!
 Four corners to my bed,
 Five angels there lie spread;
  Two at my head,
  Two at my feet,
 One at my heart, my soul to keep.

JENNY WREN

 Jenny Wren fell sick;
  Upon a merry time,
 In came Robin Redbreast,
  And brought her sops of wine.

 Eat well of the sop, Jenny,
  Drink well of the wine;
 Thank you Robin kindly,
  You shall be mine.

Jenny she got well,
　　And stood|upōn|her feet,
And told Robin plainly
　　She loved him not a bit.

Robin, being angry,
　　Hopp'd on a twig,
Saying, Out upon you,
　　Fye upon you,
　　　　Bold-faced jig!

CURLY LOCKS

Curly locks! Curly locks!
　　Wilt thou be mine?
Thou shalt not wash dishes
　　Nor yet feed the swine.
But sit on a cushion
　　And sew a fine seam,
And feed upon strawberries
　　Sugar and cream.

PUSSY-CAT MEW

Pussy-cat Mew jumped over a coal,
And in her best petticoat burnt a great hole.
Pussy-cat Mew shall have no more milk
Till she has mended her gown of silk.

DRAW A PAIL OF WATER

Draw a pail of water
For my Lady's daughter.
Father's a King,
Mother's a Queen,
My two little sisters are dressed in green,
Stamping marigolds and parsley.

I SAW A SHIP A-SAILING

I saw a ship a-sailing,
  A-sailing on the sea;
And it was full of pretty things
  For baby and for me.

There were sweetmeats in the cabin,
  And apples in the hold;
The sails were made of silk,
  And the masts were made of gold.

The four-and-twenty sailors
  That stood between the decks,
Were four-and-twenty white mice,
  With chains about their necks.

The captain was a duck,
  With a packet on his back;
And when the ship began to move,
  The captain cried, "Quack, quack!"

THE NUT-TREE

I had a little nut-tree,
  Nothing would it bear
But a silver nutmeg
  And a golden pear;
The King of Spain's daughter
  She came to see me,
And all because of my little nut-tree.
I skipped over water,
  I danced over sea,
And all the birds in the air couldn't catch me.

MY MAID MARY

My maid Mary she minds the dairy,
  While I go a-hoeing and a-mowing each
      morn;
Gaily run the reel and the little spinning-
      wheel,
  Whilst I am singing and mowing my corn.

THE WIND AND THE FISHERMAN

When the wind is in the East,
'Tis neither good for man or beast;
When the wind is in the North,
The skilful fisher goes not forth;
When the wind is in the South,
It blows the bait in the fish's mouth;
When the wind is in the West,
Then 'tis at the very best.

BLOW, WIND, BLOW

Blow, wind, blow! and go, mill, go!
   That the miller may grind his corn;
That the baker may take it and into rolls make it,
   And send us some hot in the morn.

ALL BUSY

The cock's on the house-top,
   Blowing his horn;
The bull's in the barn,
   A-threshing of corn;
The maids in the meadows
   Are making the hay,
The ducks in the river
   Are swimming away.

WINTER HAS COME

Cold and raw
  The north wind doth blow
    Bleak in the morning early;
  All the hills are covered with snow,
    And winter's now come fairly.

POOR ROBIN

  The north wind doth blow,
  And we shall have snow,
And what will poor Robin do then, poor thing?
  He'll sit in the barn,
  And keep himself warm,
And hide his head under his wing, poor thing!

I HAVE A LITTLE SISTER

I have a little sister, they call her Peep, Peep,
She wades the waters, deep, deep, deep;
She climbs the mountains, high, high, high;
Poor little creature, she has but one eye.
                (A star.)

IN MARBLE WALLS

> In marble walls as white as milk,
> Lined with a skin as soft as silk,
> Within a fountain crystal-clear,
> A golden apple doth appear.
> No doors there are to this stronghold,
> Yet thieves break in and steal the gold.
>
> (An egg.)

FAMILIAR OBJECTS

Here are some poems about things with which we are all quite familiar : the Moon and the Stars that we see through our bedroom window: Pussy purring on the hearthrug, the spotted shell on the mantelpiece.

THE MOON

> O, look at the moon!
>   She is shining up there;
> O mother, she looks
>   Like a lamp in the air.
>
> Last week she was smaller,
>   And shaped like a bow;
> But now she's grown bigger,
>   And round as an O.

Pretty moon, pretty moon,
   How you shine on the door,
And make it all bright
   On my nursery floor!

You shine on my playthings,
   And show me their place,
And I love to look up
   At your pretty bright face.

And there is a star
   Close by you, and maybe
That small twinkling star
   Is your little baby.

                ELIZA LEE FOLLEN.

THE STAR

Twinkle, twinkle, little star,
How I wonder what you are!
Up above the world so high,
Like a diamond in the sky.

When the blazing sun is gone,
When he nothing shines upon,
Then you show your little light,
Twinkle, twinkle, all the night.

Then the traveller in the dark
Thanks you for your tiny spark;
He could not see which way to go,
If you did not twinkle so.

In the dark blue sky you keep,
And often through my curtains peep,
For you never shut your eye
Till the sun is in the sky.

As your bright and tiny spark
Lights the traveller in the dark,
Though I know not what you are,
Twinkle, twinkle, little star.

ANN AND JANE TAYLOR.

KITTY

Once there was a little kitty
  Whiter than snow;
In a barn she used to frolic,
  Long time ago.

In the barn a little mousie
  Ran to and fro;
For she heard the kitty coming,
  Long time ago.

Two eyes had little kitty,
  Black as a sloe;
And they spied the little mousie,
  Long time ago.

Four paws had little kitty,
  Paws soft as dough,
And they caught the little mousie,
  Long time ago.

Nine teeth had little kitty,
  All in a row;
And they bit the little mousie,
  Long time ago.

When the teeth bit little mousie,
  Little mouse cried "Oh!"
But she got away from kitty,
  Long time ago.

                              Mrs E. Prentiss.

KITTY: How to Treat Her

I like little Pussy, her coat is so warm,
And if I don't hurt her she'll do me no harm;
So I'll not pull her tail, nor drive her away,
But Pussy and I very gently will play.

Kitty: what She thinks of Herself

I am the Cat of Cats. I am
   The everlasting cat!
Cunning, and old, and sleek as jam,
   The everlasting cat!
I hunt the vermin in the night—
   The everlasting cat!
For I see best without the light—
   The everlasting cat!

            W. B. Rands.

The Sea Shell

   Sea Shell, Sea Shell,
Sing me a song, O please!
A song of ships and sailor-men,
   Of parrots and tropical trees;
Of islands lost in the Spanish Main
Which no man ever may see again,
Of fishes and corals under the waves,
And sea-horses stabled in great green caves—
   Sea Shell, Sea Shell,
   Sing me a song, O please!

           Amy Lowell.

COUNTRY BOYS' SONGS

The Cuckoo

The cuckoo's a bonny bird,
  She sings as she flies;
She brings us good tidings,
  And tells us no lies.
She sucks little birds' eggs,
  To make her voice clear,
And never cries Cuckoo
  Till the spring of the year.

The Bird-Scarer's Song

We've ploughed our land, we've sown our seed,
We've made all neat and gay;
Then take a bit and leave a bit,
Away, birds, away!

Cradle Song

Sleep, baby, sleep,
Our cottage vale is deep;
The little lamb is on the green,
With woolly fleece so soft and clean,
Sleep, baby, sleep!

Sleep, baby, sleep,
Down where the woodbines creep;
Be always like the lamb so mild,
A kind and sweet and gentle child,
Sleep, baby, sleep!

GOOD NIGHT!

Little baby, lay your head
On your pretty cradle-bed;
Shut your eye-peeps, now the day
And the light are gone (away);
All the clothes are tucked in tight;
Little baby dear, good night.

Yes, my darling, well I know
How the bitter wind doth blow;
And the winter's snow and rain
Patter on the window-pane:
But they cannot come in here,
To my little baby dear.

For the window shutteth fast,
Till the stormy night is past;
And the curtains warm are spread
Round about her cradle-bed:
So till morning shineth bright
Little baby dear, good night!

ANN AND JANE TAYLOR.

For Those a Little Older

A BUNCH OF LENT LILIES

Here three Poets treat the same flower each from his own distinct and delightful point of view. To the first it appeals as the flower of courage, the brave early comer; to the second it is the early goer, the flower of a too swift departure—though daffodils really bloom for a fairly long time, as flowers go; the third is grateful for an imperishable recollection.

DAFFODILS

> ...Daffodils
> That come before the swallow dares, and take
> The winds of March with beauty.

SHAKESPEARE.

To DAFFODILS

> Fair daffodils, we weep to see
>   You haste away so soon;
> As yet the early-rising sun
>   Has not attain'd his noon.
>   Stay, stay
>   Until the hasting day
>   Has run
>   But to the evensong;
> And, having pray'd together, we
>   Will go with you along.

We have short time to stay, as you,
  We have as short a spring;
As quick a growth to meet decay,
  As you, or anything.
    We die
As your hours do, and dry
    Away
Like to the summer's rain;
Or as the pearls of morning's dew,
  Ne'er to be found again!

ROBERT HERRICK.

DAFFODILS

I wander'd lonely as a cloud
  That floats on high o'er vales and hills,
When all at once I saw a crowd,
  A host, of golden daffodils;
Beside the lake, beneath the trees,
Fluttering and dancing in the breeze.

Continuous as the stars that shine
  And twinkle on the Milky Way,
They stretch'd in never-ending line
  Along the margin of a bay:
Ten thousand saw I at a glance,
Tossing their heads in sprightly dance.

The waves beside them danced, but they
  Outdid the sparkling waves in glee:
A poet could not but be gay,
  In such a jocund company:
I gazed—and gazed—but little thought
What wealth the show to me had brought:

For oft, when on my couch I lie
  In vacant or in pensive mood,
They flash upon that inward eye
  Which is the bliss of solitude;
And then my heart with pleasure fills,
And dances with the daffodils.

                    WILLIAM WORDSWORTH.

SEASONS AND WEATHER

THE MONTHS

January brings the snow,
Makes our feet and fingers glow.

February brings the rain,
Thaws the frozen lake again.

March brings breezes loud and shrill,
Stirs the dancing daffodil.

April brings the primrose sweet,
Scatters daisies at our feet.

May brings flocks of pretty lambs,
Skipping by their fleecy dams.

June brings tulips, lilies, roses,
Fills the children's hands with posies.

Hot July brings cooling showers,
Apricots and gillyflowers.

August brings the sheaves of corn,
Then the harvest home is borne.

Warm September brings the fruit,
Sportsmen then begin to shoot.

Fresh October brings the pheasant,
Then to gather nuts is pleasant.

Dull November brings the blast,
Then the leaves are whirling fast.

Chill December brings the sleet,
Blazing fire and Christmas treat.

SARA COLERIDGE.

The Wind in a Frolic

The wind one morning sprang up from sleep,
Saying, "Now for a frolic! now for a leap!
Now for a madcap galloping chase!
I'll make a commotion in every place!"
So it swept with a bustle right through a great
    town,
Creaking the signs and scattering down
Shutters; and whisking, with merciless squalls,
Old women's bonnets and gingerbread stalls.
There never was heard a much lustier shout,
As the apples and oranges trundled about;
And the urchins, that stand with their thievish
    eyes
For ever on watch, ran off each with a prize.

Then away to the field it went blustering and
    humming,
And the cattle all wondered whatever was
    coming.
It plucked by their tails the grave matronly cows,
And tossed the colts' manes all about their
    brows,
Till, offended at such a familiar salute,
They all turned their backs, and stood sullenly
    mute.

2—2

So on it went, capering and playing its pranks;
Whistling with reeds on the broad river's
    banks;
Puffing the birds as they sat on the spray,
Or the traveller grave on the king's highway.
It was not too nice to hustle the bags
Of the beggar, and flutter his dirty rags;
'Twas so bold that it feared not to play its
    joke
With the doctor's wig, or the gentleman's
    cloak.
Through the forest it roared, and cried gaily,
    "Now,
You sturdy old oaks, I'll make you bow!"
And it made them bow without more ado,
Or it cracked their great branches through
    and through.

Then it rushed like a monster on cottage and
    farm,
Striking their dwellers with sudden alarm;
And they ran out like bees in a midsummer
    swarm.
There were dames with their kerchiefs tied
    over their caps,
To see if their poultry were free from mishaps;

nice : particular.

The turkeys they gobbled, the geese screamed
    aloud,
And the hens crept to roost in a terrified
    crowd;
There was rearing of ladders, and logs laying
    on
Where the thatch from the roof threatened
    soon to be gone.
But the wind had passed on, and had met in a
    lane
With a schoolboy, who panted and struggled
    in vain;
For it tossed him and twirled him, then passed,
    and he stood
With his hat in a pool and his shoe in the
    mud.

But away went the wind in its holiday glee,
And now it was far on the billowy sea,
And the lordly ships felt its staggering blow,
And the little boats darted to and fro.
But lo! it was night, and it sank to rest,
On the sea-bird's rock in the gleaming West,
Laughing to think, in its fearful fun,
How little of mischief it had done.

WILLIAM HOWITT.

THE FOUR SWEET MONTHS

First, April, she with mellow showers
Opens the way for early flowers;
Then after her comes smiling May,
In a more sweet and rich array;
Next enters June, and brings us more
Gems than those two that went before:
Then, lastly, July comes and she
More wealth brings in than all those three.

ROBERT HERRICK.

GLAD DAY

Here's another day, dear,
Here's the sun again
Peeping in his pleasant way
Through the window pane.
Rise and let him in, dear,
Hail him "hip hurray!"
Now the fun will all begin.
Here's another day!

Down the coppice path, dear,
Through the dewy glade,
(When the Morning took her bath
What a splash she made!)

Up the wet wood-way, dear,
Under dripping green
Run to meet another day,
Brightest ever seen.

Mushrooms in the field, dear,
Show their silver gleam.
What a dainty crop they yield
Firm as clouted cream,
Cool as balls of snow, dear,
Sweet and fresh and round!
Ere the early dew can go
We must clear the ground.

Such a lot to do, dear,
Such a lot to see!
How we ever can get through
Fairly puzzles me.
Hurry up and out, dear,
Then—away! away!
In and out and round about,
Here's another day!

W. GRAHAM ROBERTSON.

BUTTERCUPS AND DAISIES

Buttercups and daisies—
O the pretty flowers!
Coming ere the spring-time,
  To tell of sunny hours.
When the trees are leafless;
  When the fields are bare;
Buttercups and daisies
  Spring up here and there.

Welcome, yellow buttercups!
Welcome, daisies white!
Ye are in my spirit
  Vision'd, a delight!
Coming ere the spring-time,
  Of sunny hours to tell—
Speaking to our hearts of Him
  Who doeth all things well.

MARY HOWITT.

THE MERRY MONTH OF MARCH

The cock is crowing,
The stream is flowing,
The small birds twitter,
The lake doth glitter,
The green field sleeps in the sun;

The oldest and youngest
Are at work with the strongest;
The cattle are grazing,
Their heads never raising;
There are forty feeding like one!

Like an army defeated
The snow hath retreated,
And now doth fare ill
On the top of the bare hill;
The Plough-boy is whooping anon, anon.
There's joy in the mountains;
There's life in the fountains;
Small clouds are sailing,
Blue sky prevailing;
The rain is over and gone!

WILLIAM WORDSWORTH.

WHAT THE BIRDS SAY

Do you know what the birds say?   The
    sparrow, the dove,
The linnet and thrush say "I love and I love!"
In the winter they're silent—the wind is so
    strong;
What it says I don't know, but it sings a loud
    song.

But green leaves, and blossoms, and sunny
    warm weather,
And singing, and loving, all come back together.
But the lark is so brimful of gladness and love,
The green fields below him, the blue sky above,
That he sings, and he sings, and for ever-sings
    he—
"I love my love, and my love loves me!"

                     S. T. COLERIDGE.

SPRING'S PROCESSION

    First came the primrose, .
    On the bank high,
    Like a maiden looking forth
    From the window of a tower
    When the battle rolls below,
    So look'd she,
    And saw the storms go by.

    Then came the wind=flower
    In the valley left behind,
    As a wounded maiden, pale
    With purple streaks of woe,
    When the battle has roll'd by
    Wanders to and fro,
    So tottered she,
    Dishevell'd in the wind.

Then came the daisies,
On the first of May,
Like a banner'd show's advance
While the crowd runs by the way,
With ten thousand flowers about them
    they came trooping through the fields.
As a happy people come,
So came they,
As a happy people come
When the war has roll'd away,
With dance and tabor, pipe and drum,
And all make holiday.

Then came the cowslip,
Like a dancer in the fair,
She spread her little mat of green,
And on it danced she.
With a fillet bound about her brow,
A fillet round her happy brow,
A golden fillet round her brow,
And rubies in her hair.

SYDNEY DOBELL.

THE CALL OF THE WOODS

> Under the greenwood tree,
> Who loves to lie with me,
> And tune his merry note
> Unto the sweet bird's throat,
> Come hither, come hither, come hither!
> Here shall he see
> No enemy
> But winter and rough weather.

> Who doth ambition shun,
> And loves to live in the sun,
> Seeking the food he eats,
> And pleas'd with what he gets,
> Come hither, come hither, come hither!
> Here shall he see
> No enemy
> But winter and rough weather.

SHAKESPEARE.

A PRESCRIPTION FOR A SPRING MORNING

At early dawn through London you must go
Until you come where long black hedgerows
    grow,
With pink buds pearl'd, with here and there a
    tree,

And gates and stiles; and watch good
    country folk;
And scent the spicy smoke
Of wither'd weeds that burn where gardens be;
And in a ditch perhaps a primrose see.
The rooks shall stalk the plough, larks mount
    the skies,
    Blackbirds and speckled thrushes sing aloud,
    Hid in the warm white cloud
Mantling the thorn, and far away shall rise
The milky low of cows and farm-yard cries.

From windy heavens the climbing sun shall
    shine,
    And February greet you like a maid
    In russet cloak array'd;
And you shall take her for your mistress fine,
And pluck a crocus for her valentine.

                    JOHN DAVIDSON.

THE COUNTRY FAITH

    Here in the country's heart
    Where the grass is green,
    Life is the same sweet life
    As it e'er hath been

Trust in a God still lives,
And the bell at morn
Floats with a thought of God
O'er the rising corn.

God comes down in the rain,
And the crop grows tall—
This is the country faith,
And the best of all.

NORMAN GALE.

THE BUTTERFLY'S BALL

"Come, take up your hats, and away let us
haste
To the Butterfly's Ball and the Grasshopper's
Feast;
The Trumpeter, Gadfly, has summoned the
crew,
And the revels are now only waiting for you."
So said little Robert, and pacing along,
His merry Companions came forth in a throng,
And on the smooth Grass by the side of a Wood,
Beneath a broad oak that for ages had stood,
Saw the Children of Earth and the Tenants of
Air
For an Evening's Amusement together repair.

And there came the Beetle, so blind and so
black,
Who carried the Emmet, his friend, on his
back.
And there was the Gnat and the Dragon-fly too,
With all their Relations, green, orange and blue.
And there came the Moth, with his plumage
of down,
And the Hornet in jacket of yellow and brown;
Who with him the Wasp, his companion, did
bring,
But they promised that evening to lay by
their sting.
And the sly little Dormouse crept out of his
hole,
And brought to the feast his blind Brother,
the Mole,
And the Snail, with his horns peeping out of
his shell,
Came from a great distance, the length of an
ell.

A Mushroom their Table, and on it was laid
A water-dock leaf, which a table-cloth made.
The Viands were various, to each of their taste,
And the Bee brought her honey to crown the
Repast.

Then close on his haunches, so solemn and wise,
The Frog from a corner look'd up to the skies;
And the Squirrel, well pleased such diversions
    to see,
Mounted high overhead and look'd down from
    a tree.

Then out came the Spider, with finger so fine,
To show his dexterity on the tight-line.
From one branch to another his cobwebs he
    slung,
Then quick as an arrow he darted along.
But just in the middle—oh! shocking to tell,
From his rope, in an instant, poor Harlequin
    fell.
Yet he touched not the ground, but with
    talons outspread,
Hung suspended in air, at the end of a thread.

Then the Grasshopper came, with a jerk and a
    spring,
Very long was his leg, though but short was
    his Wing;
He took but three leaps, and was soon out of
    sight,
Then chirp'd his own praises the rest of the
    night.

With step so majestic the Snail did advance,
And promised the Gazers a Minuet to dance;
But they all laughed so loud that he pulled in
  his head,
And went in his own little chamber to bed.
Then as Evening gave way to the shadows of
  Night,
Their Watchman, the Glowworm, came out
  with a light.

"Then home let us hasten, while yet we can
  see,
For no Watchman is waiting for you and for
  me."
So said little Robert, and pacing along,
His merry Companions return'd in a throng.

WILLIAM ROSCOE.

TASTES AND PREFERENCES

A WISH

  Mine be a cot beside the hill;
    A bee-hive's hum shall soothe my ear;
  A willowy brook, that turns a mill,
    With many a fall shall linger near.

The swallow oft beneath my thatch
   Shall twitter from her clay-built nest;
Oft shall the pilgrim lift the latch
   And share my meal, a welcome guest.

Around my ivied porch shall spring
   Each fragrant flower that drinks the dew;
And Lucy at her wheel shall sing
   In russet gown and apron blue.

The village church among the trees,
   Where first our marriage vows were given,
With merry peals shall swell the breeze,
   And point with taper spire to Heaven.

                  SAMUEL ROGERS.

WISHING

Ring-ting! I wish I were a Primrose,
A bright yellow Primrose blowing in the
     Spring!
   The stooping boughs above me,
   The wandering bee to love me,
The fern and moss to creep across,
    And the Elm-tree for our King!

Nay—stay! I wish I were an Elm-tree, ·
A great lofty Elm-tree, with green leaves gay!
    The winds would set them dancing,
    The sun and moonshine glance in,
The birds would house among the boughs,
      And sweetly sing!

O—no! I wish I were a Robin,
A Robin or a little Wren, everywhere to go;
    Through forest, field, or garden,
    And ask no leave or pardon,
Till Winter comes with icy thumbs
      To ruffle up our wing!

Well—tell! Where should I fly to,
Where go to sleep in the dark wood or dell?
    Before a day was over,
    Home comes the rover,
For Mother's kiss,—sweeter this
      Than any other thing!

                WILLIAM ALLINGHAM.

BUNCHES OF GRAPES

    "Bunches of grapes," says Timothy;
    "Pomegranates pink," says Elaine;
    "A junket of cream and a cranberry tart
    For me," says Jane.

"Love-in-a-mist," says Timothy;
"Primroses pale," says Elaine;
"A nosegay of pinks and mignonette
For me," says Jane.

"Chariots of gold," says Timothy;
"Silvery wings," says Elaine;
"A bumpity ride in a waggon of hay
For me," says Jane.

WALTER RAMAL.

CONTENTMENT

Once on a time an old red hen
　　Went strutting round with pompous clucks,
For she had little babies ten,
　　A part of which were tiny ducks.
"'Tis very rare that hens," said she,
　　"Have baby ducks as well as chicks—
But I possess, as you can see,
　　Of chickens four and ducklings six!"

A season later, this old hen
　　Appeared, still cackling of her luck,
For, though she boasted babies ten,
　　Not one among them was a duck!

"'Tis well," she murmured, brooding o'er
   The little chicks of fleecy down,
"My babies now will stay ashore,
   And, consequently, cannot drown!"

The following spring the old red hen
   Clucked just as proudly as of yore—
But lo! her babes were ducklings ten,
   Instead of chickens as before!
"'Tis better," said the old red hen,
   As she surveyed her waddling brood;
"A little water now and then
   . Will surely do my darlings good!"

But oh! alas, how very sad!
   When gentle spring rolled round again,
The eggs eventuated bad,
   . And childless was the old red hen!
Yet patiently she bore her woe,
   And still she wore a cheerful air,
And said: "'Tis best these things are so,
   For babies are a dreadful care!"

I half suspect that many men,
   And many, many women too,
Could learn a lesson from the hen
   With plumage of vermilion hue.

She ne'er presumed to take offence
  At any fate that might befāll,
But meekly bowed to Providence—
  She was contented—that was all!

                    EUGENE FIELD.

TOYS AND PLAY, IN-DOORS AND OUT

THE LAND OF STORY-BOOKS

At evening when the lamp is lit,
Around the fire my parents sit;
They sit at home and talk and sing,
And do not play at anything.

Now, with my little gun, I crawl
All in the dark along the wall,
And follow round the forest track
Away behind the sofa back.

There, in the night, where none can spy,
All in my hunter's camp I lie,
And play at books that I have read
Till it is time to go to bed.

These are the hills, these are the woods,
These are my starry solitudes;
And there the river by whose brink
The roaring lions come to drink.

I see the others far away
As if in firelit camp they lay,
And I, like to an Indian scout,
Around their party prowled about.

So, when my nurse comes in for me,
Home I return across the sea,
And go to bed with backward looks
At my dear land of Story-books.

R. L. STEVENSON.

SAND CASTLES

Build me a castle of sand
    Down by the sea.
Here on the edge of the strand
    Build it for me.
How shall a foeman invade,
    Where may he land,
While we can raise with our spade
    Castles of sand?

W. Graham Robertson

Turrets upleap and aspire,
  Battlements rise
Sweeping the sea with their fire,
  Storming the skies.
Pile that a monarch might own,
  Mightily plann'd!
I can't sit here on a throne,
  This is too grand.

Build me a cottage of sand
  Up on the hill;
Snug in a cleft it must stand
  Sunny and still.
Plant it with ragwort and ling,
  Bramble and bine:
Castles I'll leave to the King,
  This shall be mine.

Storm-clouds drive over the land,
  High flies the spray;
Gone are our houses of sand,
  Vanished away!
Look at the damage you've done,
  Sea-wave and rain!
—"Nay, we but give you your fun
  Over again."

W. Graham Robertson.

Ring o' Roses

Hush a while, my darling, for the long day
    closes,
  Nodding into slumber on the blue hill's crest.
See the little clouds play Ring a ring o' roses,
  Planting Fairy gardens in the red-rose West.

Greet him for us, cloudlets, say we're not for-
    getting
  Golden gifts of sunshine, merry hours of
    play.
Ring a ring o' roses round the sweet sun's
    setting,
  Spread a bed of roses for the dear dead day.

Hush-a-bye, my little one, the dear day dozes,
  Doffed his crown of kingship and his fair
    flag furled,
While the earth and sky play Ring a ring o'
    roses,
  Ring a ring o' roses round the rose-red world.

                    W. Graham Robertson.

DREAM-LAND

WYNKEN, BLYNKEN, AND NOD

Wynken, Blynken, and Nod one night
  Sailed off in a wooden shoe—
Sailed on a river of crystal light,
  Into a sea of dew.
"Where are you going, and what do you
    wish?"
  The old moon asked the three.
"We have come to fish for the herring fish
  That live in this beautiful sea;
  Nets of silver and gold have we!"
          Said Wynken,
          Blynken,
          And Nod.

The old moon laughed and sang a song,
  As they rocked in the wooden shoe,
And the wind that sped them all night long
  Ruffled the waves of dew.
The little stars were the herring fish
  That lived in that beautiful sea—
"Now cast your nets wherever you wish—
  Never afeared are we":
  So cried the stars to the fishermen three:
          Wynken,
          Blynken,
          And Nod.

All night long their nets they threw
 To the stars in the twinkling foam—
Then down from the skies came the wooden shoe,
 Bringing the fishermen home;
'Twas all so pretty a sail it seemed
 As if it could not be,
And some folks thought 'twas a dream they'd
 dreamed
 Of sailing that beautiful sea—
 But I shall name you the fishermen three:
 Wynken,
 Blynken,
 And Nod.

Wynken and Blynken are two little eyes,
 And Nod is a little head,
And the wooden shoe that sailed the skies
 Is a wee one's trundle-bed.
So shut your eyes while mother sings
 Of wonderful sights that be,
And you shall see the beautiful things
 As you rock in the misty sea,
 Where the old shoe rocked the fishermen
 three:
 Wynken,
 Blynken,
 And Nod.
 EUGENE FIELD.

THE DRUMMER-BOY AND THE SHEPHERDESS

Drummer-boy, drummer-boy, where is your
    drum?
And why do you weep, sitting here on your
    thumb?
The soldiers are out, and the fifes we can hear;
But where is the drum of the young grenadier?

"My dear little drum it was stolen away
Whilst I was asleep on a sunshiny day;
It was all through the drone of a big bumble-
    bee,
And sheep and a shepherdess under a tree."

Shepherdess, shepherdess, where is your crook?
And why is your little lamb over the brook?
It bleats for its dam, and dog Tray is not by,
So why do you stand with a tear in your eye?

"My dear little crook it was stolen away
Whilst I dreamt a dream on a morning in May;
It was all through the drone of a big bumble-
    bee,
And a drum and a drummer-boy under a tree."

                                        W. B. RANDS.

THE LAND OF DREAMS

"Awake, awake, my little boy!
Thou wast thy mother's only joy;
Why dost thou weep in thy gentle sleep?
O wake! thy father doth thee keep.

O what land is the land of dreams?
What are its mountains and what are its
    streams?"
"O father! I saw my mother there,
Among the lilies by waters fair."

"Dear child! I also by pleasant streams
Have wandered all night in the land of dreams,
But, though calm and warm the waters wide
I could not get to the other side."

"Father, O father! what do we here,
In this land of unbelief and fear?
The land of dreams is better far,
Above the light of the morning star."

                WILLIAM BLAKE.

SWEET AND LOW

Sweet and low, sweet and low,
Wind of the western sea,
Low, low, breathe and blow,
  Wind of the western sea!

Over the rolling waters go,
Come from the dying moon, and blow,
  Blow him again to me;
While my little one, while my pretty one,
    sleeps.

Sleep and rest, sleep and rest,
  Father will come to thee soon;
Rest, rest, on mother's breast,
  Father will come to thee soon;
Father will come to his babe in the nest,
Silver sails all out of the west
  Under the silver moon:
Sleep, my little one, sleep, my pretty one, sleep.

ALFRED, LORD TENNYSON.

CRADLE SONG

O hush thee, my baby, thy sire was a knight,
Thy mother a lady, both lovely and bright;
The woods and the glens, from the towers which
    we see,
They all are belonging, dear baby, to thee.

O fear not the bugle, though loudly it blows,
It calls but the warders that guard thy repose;
Their bows would be bended, their blades
    would be red,
Ere the step of a foeman draws near to thy bed.

O hush thee, my baby, the time will soon come,
When thy sleep shall be broken by trumpet
    and drum;
Then hush thee, my darling, take rest while
    you may,
For strife comes with manhood, and waking
    with day.

Sir Walter Scott.

Mother and I

O Mother-My-Love, if you'll give me your hand,
    And go where I ask you to wander,
I will lead you away to a beautiful land—
    The Dreamland that's waiting out yonder.
We'll walk in a sweet-posy garden out there,
    Where moonlight and starlight are streaming,
And the flowers and the birds are filling the air
    With the fragrance and music of dreaming.

There'll be no little tired-out boy to undress,
    No questions or cares to perplex you;
There'll be no little bruises or bumps to caress,
    Nor patching of stockings to vex you.
For I'll rock you away on a silver-dew stream,
    And sing you asleep when you're weary,
And no one shall know of our beautiful dream
    But you and your own little dearie.

And when I am tired I'll nestle my head
  In the bosom that's sooth'd me so often,
And the wide-awake stars shall sing in my
    stead
  A song which our dreaming shall soften.
So Mother-My-Love, let me take your dear
    hand,
  And away through the starlight we'll
  wander—
Away through the mist to the beautiful land—
  The Dreamland that's waiting out yonder!

EUGENE FIELD.

FAIRY-LAND

THE FAIRIES

Up the airy mountain,
  Down the rushy glen,
We daren't go a-hunting
  For fear of little men;
Wee folk, good folk,
Trooping all together;
Green jacket, red cap,
  And white owl's feather!

Down along the rocky shore
  Some make their home,
They live on crispy pancakes
  Of yellow tide-foam;
Some in the reeds
  Of the black mountain-lake,
With frogs for their watch-dogs,
  All night awake.

High on the hill-top
  The old King sits;
He is now so old and grey
  He's nigh lost his wits.
With a bridge of white mist
  Columbkill he crosses,
On his stately journeys
  From Slieveleague to Rosses;
Or going up with music
  On cold starry nights,
To sup with the Queen
  Of the gay Northern Lights.

They stole little Bridget
  For seven years long;
When she came down again
  Her friends were all gone.

They took her lightly back,
  Between the night and morrow,
They thought that she was fast asleep,
  But she was dead with sorrow.
They have kept her ever since
  Deep within the lakes,
On a bed of flag-leaves,
  Watching till she wakes.

By the craggy hill-side,
  Through the mosses bare,
They have planted thorn-trees
  For pleasure here and there.
Is any man so daring
  As dig one up in spite,
He shall find their sharpest thorns
  In his bed at night.

Up the airy mountain,
  Down the rushy glen,
We daren't go a-hunting
  For fear of little men;
Wee folk, good folk,
  Trooping all together,
Green jacket, red cap,
  And white owl's feather!

                    WILLIAM ALLINGHAM.

SHAKESPEARE'S FAIRIES

Some of them,—

Ye elves of hills, brooks, standing lakes and
  groves,
And ye that on the sands with printless foot
Do chase the ebbing Neptune and do fly him
When he comes back; you demi-puppets, that
By moonshine do the green sour ringlets make
Whereof the ewe not bites, and you whose
  pastime
Is to make midnight mushrooms, that rejoice
To hear the solemn curfew....

They Dance and Play,—

  Come unto these yellow sands,
    And then take hands:
  Courtsied when you have, and kiss'd,—
    The wild waves whist,—
  Foot it featly here and there;
    And, sweet sprites, the burthen bear.

> *Demi-puppets :* half the size of a doll.
> *Whist ·* silent.
> *Featly :* neatly, elegantly.

4—2

Hark, hark!
> *Bow, wow,*
The watch-dogs bark:
> *Bow, wow,*
Hark, hark! I hear
The strain of strutting chanticleer
Cry, Cock-a-diddle-dow!

Ariel Sings,—
Where the bee sucks, there suck I:
  In a cowslip's bell I lie;
There I couch when owls do cry.
On the bat's back I do fly
After summer merrily.
  Merrily, merrily, shall I live now,
  Under the blossom that hangs on the boug

A Busy One
  Over hill, over dale,
    Thorough bush, thorough brier,
  Over park, over pale,
    Thorough flood, thorough fire,
    I do wander everywhere,
    Swifter than the moonè's sphere;
    And I serve the fairy queen,
    To dew her orbs upon the green.

  Orbs : circles, or fairy rings.

The cowslips tall her pensioners be;
In their gold coats spots you see;
Those be rubies, fairy favours,
In those freckles live their savours:
I must go seek some dewdrops here, ·
And hang a pearl in every cowslip's ear.

They Sing Their Queen to Sleep,—
You spotted snakes with double tongue,
Thorny hedgehogs, be not seen;
Newts and blind-worms, do no wrong;
Come not near our fairy queen.
Philomel, with melody
Sing in our sweet lullaby;
Lulla, lulla, lullaby; lulla, lulla, lullaby!
Never harm,
Nor spell nor charm,
Come our lovely lady nigh;
So, good night, with lullaby.

Weaving spiders, come not here;
Hence, you long-legg'd spinners, hence!
Beetles black, approach not near;
Worm nor snail, do no offence.
Philomel, with melody,
Sing in our sweet lullaby;
Lulla, lulla, lullaby; lulla, lulla, lullaby!

> Never harm,
>   Nor spell nor charm,
> Come our lovely lady nigh;
> So, good night, with lullaby.

SHAKESPEARE.

THE LAVENDER BEDS

The garden was pleasant with old-fashioned
    flowers,
The sunflowers and hollyhocks stood up like
    towers;
There were dark turncap lilies and jessamine
    rare,
And sweet thyme and marjoram scented the air.

The moon made the sun-dial tell the time
    wrong;
'Twas too late in the year for the nightingale's
    song;
The box-trees were clipped, and the alleys were
    straight,
Till you came to the shrubbery hard by the gate.

The fairies stepped out of the lavender beds,
With mob-caps, or wigs, on their quaint little
    heads;
My lord had a sword and my lady a fan;
The music struck up and the dancing began.

I watched them go through with a grave
    minuet;
Wherever they footed the dew was not wet;
They bowed and they curtsied, the brave and
    the fair;
And laughter like chirping of crickets was
    there.

Then all on a sudden a church clock struck loud:
A flutter, a shiver, was seen in the crowd,
The cock crew, the wind woke, the trees tossed
    their heads,
And the fairy folk hid in the lavender beds.

W. B. RANDS.

FAREWELL TO THE FAIRIES

Farewell rewards and fairies,
    Good housewives now may say,
For now foul sluts in dairies
    Do fare as well as they.
And though they sweep their hearths no less
    Than maids were wont to do,
Yet who of late, for cleanliness,
    Finds sixpence in her shoe?

At morning and at evening both,
　　You merry were and glad,
So little care of sleep or sloth
　　Those pretty ladies had.
When Tom came home from labour,
　　Or Cis to milking rose,
Then merrily went their tabor,
　　And nimbly went their toes.

Witness those rings and roundelays
　　Of theirs, which yet remain,
Were footed in Queen Mary's days
　　On many a grassy plain;
But since of late Elizabeth,
　　And later, James came in,
They never danced on any heath
　　As when the time hath been.

By which we note the fairies
　　Were of the old profession,
Their songs were Ave-Maries,
　　Their dances were procession:
But now, alas! they all are dead,
　　Or gone beyond the seas;
Or farther for religion fled,
　　Or else they take their ease.

A tell-tale in their company
  They never could endure,
And whoso kept not secretly
  Their mirth, was punished sure;
It was a just and Christian deed
  To pinch such black and blue:
O how the commonwealth doth need
  Such justices as you!
          Richard Corbet (1582—1635).

Dirge on the Death of Oberon, the
Fairy King

  Toll the lilies' silver bells!
    Oberon, the King, is dead!
  In her grief the crimson rose
    All her velvet leaves has shed.

  Toll the lilies' silver bells!
    Oberon is dead and gone!
  He who looked an emperor
    When his glow-worm crown was on.

  Toll the lilies' silver bells!
    Slay the dragonfly, his steed;
  Dig his grave within the ring
    Of the mushrooms in the mead.
                G. W. Thornbury.

(But he wasn't dead really. It was all a mist.'ke.
So they didn't slay the dragonfly after all.)

KILMENY

(A Story about one who went there)

Bonny Kilmeny gaed up the glen;
But it wasna to meet Duneira's men,
Nor the rosy monk of the isle to see,
For Kilmeny was pure as pure could be.
It was only to hear the yorlin sing,
And pull the blue cress-flower round the spring;
To pull the hip and the hindberrye,
And the nut that hung frae the hazel-tree;
For Kilmeny was pure as pure could be.
But lang may her minnie look o'er the wa',
And lang may she seek in the greenwood shaw;
Lang the Laird·o' Duneira blame,
And lang, lang greet e'er Kilmeny come hame!
When many a day had come and fled,
When grief grew calm, and hope was dead,
When mass for Kilmeny's soul had been sung,
When the bedesman had prayed and the dead-
      bell rung;
Late, late in a gloaming, when all was still,
When the fringe was red on the westlin hill,
The wood was sere, the moon i' the wane,
The reek of the cot hung o'er the plain,

gaed : went.   *yorlin :* yellow-hammer.   *bindberrye :* wild
raspberry. *minnie :* mother. *greet :* weep. *westlin :* western.
reek : smoke.

Like a little wee cloud in the world its lane;
When the ingle lowed with an eery gleam,
Late, late in the gloamin', Kilmeny came hame!

"Kilmeny, Kilmeny, where have you been?
Lang hae we sought baith holt and dene;
By linn, by ford, and green-wood tree,
Yet you are halesome and fair to see.
Where gat you that joup of the lily sheen?
That bonny snood of the birk sae green?
And these roses, the fairest that ever were seen?
Kilmeny, Kilmeny, where have you been?"

Kilmeny look'd up with a lovely grace,
But nae smile was seen on Kilmeny's face;
As still was her look, and as still was her ee,
As the stillness that lay on the emerald lea,
Or the mist that sleeps on a waveless sea.
For Kilmeny had been she knew not where,
And Kilmeny had seen what she could not
    declare.
Kilmeny had been where the cock never crew,
Where the rain never fell, and the wind never
    blew.
But it seem'd as the harp of the sky had rung,
And the airs of heaven play'd round her tongue,

its lane: alone.   *ingle:* fire.   *lowed:* flamed.   *linn:* water-
fall.   *joup:* bodice.   *snood:* hair-ribbon.   *birk:* birch.

When she spake of the lovely forms she had
    seen,
And a land where sin had never been;
A land of love and a land of light,
Withouten sun, or moon, or night;
The land of vision it would seem,
And still an everlasting dream.

.   .   .   .   .   .

They lifted Kilmeny, they led her away,
And she walk'd in the light of a sunless day;
The sky was a dome of crystal bright,
The fountain of vision, and fountain of light:
The emerald fields were of dazzling glow,
And the flowers of everlasting blow.
Then deep in the stream her body they laid,
That her youth and beauty might never fade;
And they smiled on heaven, when they saw
    her lie
In the stream of life that wander'd by.
And she heard a song, she heard it sung,
She kenn'd not where; but so sweetly it rung,
It fell on the ear like a dream of the morn:
"O blest be the day Kilmeny was born!"

.   .   .   .   .   .

To sing of the sights Kilmeny saw,
So far surpassing nature's law,

The singer's voice would sink away,
And the string of his harp would cease to play.
But she saw till the sorrows of man were by,
And all was love and harmony;
Till the stars of heaven fell calmly away,
Like the flakes of snow on a winter day.

.   .   .   .   .   .

When seven lang years had come and fled,
When grief was calm and hope was dead;
When scarce was remembered Kilmeny's name,
Late, late in a gloaming Kilmeny came hame!
And O, her beauty was fair to see,
But still and steadfast was her ee!
Her seymar was the lily flower,
And her cheek the moss-rose in the shower;
And her voice like the distant melody
That floats along the twilight sea.
But she loved to raike the lanely glen,
And keepit away frae the haunts of men;
Her holy hymns unheard to sing,
To suck the flowers, and drink the spring.
But wherever her peaceful form appear'd,
The wild beasts of the hill were cheer'd;
The wolf play'd blythly round the field,
The lordly bison low'd and kneel'd;

seymar: a light robe.   *raike:* wander through.

Thè dun deer woo'd with manner bland,
And cower'd aneath her lily hand.
And all in a peaceful ring were hurl'd;
It was like an eve in a sinless world!

When a month and a day had come and gane,
Kilmeny sought the green-wood wene;
There laid her down on the leaves sae green,
And Kilmeny on earth was never mair seen.

JAMES HOGG.

TWO SONGS

A Boy's Song

Where the pools are bright and deep,
Where the grey trout lies asleep,
Up the river and over the lea,
That's the way for Billy and me.

Where the blackbird sings the latest,
Where the hawthorn blooms the sweetest,
Where the nestlings chirp and flee,
That's the way for Billy and me.

Where the mowers mow the cleanest,
Where the hay lies thick and greenest,
There to track the homeward bee,
That's the way for Billy and me.

Where the hazel bank is steepest,
Where the shadow falls the deepest,
Where the clustering nuts fall free,
That's the way for Billy and me.

Why the boys should drive away
Little sweet maidens from the play,
Or love to banter and fight so well,
That's the thing I never could tell.

But this I know, I love to play
Through the meadow, among the hay;
Up the water and over the lea,
That's the way for Billy and me.

JAMES HOGG.

A GIRL'S SONG

There's a bower of roses by Bendemeer's stream,
And the nightingale sings round it all the
day long;
In the time of my childhood 'twas like a sweet
dream
To sit in the roses and hear the bird's song.

That bower and its music I never forget,
But oft when alone in the bloom of the year,
I think—is the nightingale singing there yet?
Are the roses still bright by the calm Bende-
meer?

No, the roses soon withered that hung o'er the
    wave,
   But some blossoms were gathered, while
    freshly they shone,
And a dew was distilled from their flowers, that
    gave
   All the fragrance of summer, when summer
    was gone.
Thus memory draws from delight, ere it dies,
   An essence that breathes of it many a year;
Thus bright to my soul, as 'twas then to my
    eyes,
   Is that bower on the banks of the calm
    Bendemeer!

THOMAS MOORE.

FUR AND FEATHER

"Men are brethren of each other,
   One in flesh and one in food;
And a sort of foster brother
   Is the litter, or the brood,
Of that folk in fur or feather,
   Who, with men together,
   Breast the wind and weather."

CHRISTINA ROSSETTI.

THREE THINGS TO REMEMBER

A Robin Redbreast in a cage
Puts all Heaven in a rage.

A skylark wounded on the wing
Doth make a cherub cease to sing.

He who shall hurt the little wren
Shall never be·beloved by men.

WILLIAM BLAKE.

THE KNIGHT OF BETHLEHEM

There was a Knight of Bethlehem,
   Whose wealth was tears and sorrows;
His men-at-arms were little lambs,
   His trumpeters were sparrows.
His castle was a wooden cross,
   On which he hung so high;
His helmet was a crown of thorns,
   Whose crest did touch the sky.

H. N. MAUGHAM.

THE LAMB

Little Lamb, who made thee?
Dost thou know who made thee?
Gave thee life, and bade thee feed
By the stream and o'er the mead;

Gave thee clothing of delight,
Softest clothing, woolly, bright;
Gave thee such a tender voice,
Making all the vales rejoice?
 Little lamb, who made thee?
 Dost thou know who made thee?

 Little lamb, I'll tell thee;
 Little lamb, I'll tell thee:
He is callèd by thy name,
For He calls Himself a Lamb.
He is meek, and He is mild,
He became a little child.
I a child, and thou a lamb,
We are called by His name.
 Little lamb, God bless thee!
 Little lamb, God bless thee!

WILLIAM BLAKE.

THE TIGER

Tiger, Tiger, burning bright
In the forest of the night,
What immortal hand or eye
Framed thy fearful symmetry?

In what distant deeps or skies
Burned that fire within thine eyes?
On what wings dared he aspire?
What the hand dared seize the fire?

And what shoulder, and what art,
Could twist the sinews of thy heart?
When thy heart began to beat,
What dread hand formed thy dread feet?

What the hammer, what the chain,
Knit thy strength and forged thy brain?
What the anvil? What dread grasp
Dared thy deadly terrors clasp?

When the stars threw down their spears,
And water'd heaven with their tears,
Did He smile His work to see?
Did He who made the lamb make thee?

WILLIAM BLAKE.

I HAD A DOVE

I had a dove, and the sweet dove died;
And I have thought it died of grieving;
O, what could it grieve for? Its feet were tied
With a silken thread of my own hands'
weaving.

Sweet little red feet! why should you die—
Why would you leave me, sweet bird! why?
You lived alone in the forest tree,
Why, pretty thing! would you not live with me
I kiss'd you oft and gave you white peas;
Why not live sweetly, as in the green trees?

JOHN KEATS.

ROBIN REDBREAST

Good-bye, good-bye to Summer!
  For Summer's nearly done;
The garden smiling faintly,
  Cool breezes in the sun;
Our thrushes now are silent,
  Our swallows flown away,—
But Robin's here in coat of brown,
  And scarlet breast-knot gay.
Robin, Robin Redbreast,
  O Robin dear!
Robin sings so sweetly
  In the falling of the year.

Bright yellow, red, and orange,
  The leaves come down in hosts;
The trees are Indian princes,
  But soon they'll turn to ghosts;

The leathery pears and apples
  Hang russet on the bough;
It's Autumn, Autumn, Autumn late,
  'Twill soon be Winter now.
Robin, Robin Redbreast,
  O Robin dear!
And what will this poor Robin do?
  For pinching days are near.

The fireside for the cricket,
  The wheatstack for the mouse,
When trembling night-winds whistle
  And moan all round the house.
The frosty ways like iron,
  The branches plumed with snow,—
Alas! in winter dead and dark,
  Where can poor Robin go?
Robin, Robin Redbreast,
  O Robin dear!
And a crumb of bread for Robin,
  His little heart to cheer.

                WILLIAM ALLINGHAM.

BLACK BUNNY

It was a black Bunny, with white in its head,
Alive when the children went cosy to bed—
O early next morning that Bunny was dead!

When Bunny's young master awoke up from
    sleep,
To look at the creatures young master did creep,
And saw that this black one lay all of a heap.
"O Bunny, what ails you ? What does it import
That you lean on one side, with your breath
    coming short ?
For I never before saw a thing of the sort!"
They took him so gently up out of his hutch,
They made him a sick-bed, they loved him so
    much ;
They wrapped him up warm ; they said, Poor
    thing, and such ;
But all to no purpose. Black Bunny he died,
And rolled over limp on his little black side ;
The grown-up spectators looked awkward and
    sighed.
While, as for those others in that congregation,
You heard voices lifted in sore lamentation ;
But three-year-old Baby desired explanation :
At least, so it seemed. Then they buried their
    dead
In a nice quiet place, with a flag at his head ;
"Poor Bunny !"—in large print—was what
    the flag said.

Now, as they were shovelling the earth in the
hole,
Little Baby burst out, "I *don't* like it!"—poor
soul!
And bitterly wept.   So the dead had his dole.

That evening, as Babe she was cuddling to bed,
"The Bunny will come back again," Baby
said,
"And be a *white* bunny, and never be dead!"

W. B. RANDS.

THE COW

Thank you, pretty cow, that made
Pleasant milk to soak my bread,
Every day, and every night,
Warm, and fresh, and sweet, and white.

Do not chew the hemlock rank,
Growing on the weedy bank;
But the yellow cowslips eat,
They will make it very sweet.

Where the purple violet grows,
Where the bubbling water flows,
Where the grass is fresh and fine,
Pretty cow, go there and dine.

ANN AND JANE TAYLOR.

THE SKYLARK

Bird of the wilderness,
Blythesome and cumberless,
Sweet be thy matin o'er moorland and lea!
Emblem of happiness,
Blest is thy dwelling-place—
O to abide in the desert with thee!
Wild is thy lay and loud
Far in the downy cloud,
Love gives it energy, love gave it birth.
Where, on thy dewy wing,
Where art thou journeying?
Thy lay is in heaven, thy love is on earth.

O'er fell and fountain sheen,
O'er moor and mountain green,
O'er the red streamer that heralds the day,
Over the cloudlet dim,
Over the rainbow's rim,
Musical cherub, soar, singing, away!
Then, when the gloaming comes,
Low in the heather blooms,
Sweet will thy welcome and bed of love be!
Emblem of happiness,
Blest is thy dwelling-place—
O to abide in the desert with thee!

JAMES HOGG.

cumberless: unencumbered, free from care.

CHRISTMAS POEMS

Here one would like to have begun with some of the old-time carols. But carols, somehow, seem to demand certain accompaniments—snow and frost, starlight and lantern-light, a mingling of Church bells, and above all their own simple haunting music. In cold print they do not appeal to us to the same extent. But the poems that follow are in the true carol-spirit.

CHRISTMAS EVE

    In holly hedges starving birds
      Silently mourn the setting year;
    Upright like silver-plated swords
      The flags stand in the frozen mere.

    The mistletoe we still adore
      Upon the twisted hawthorn grows:
    In antique gardens hellebore
      Puts forth its blushing Christmas rose.

    Shrivell'd and purple, cheek by jowl,
      The hips and haws hang drearily;
    Roll'd in a ball the sulky owl
      Creeps far into his hollow tree.

In abbeys and cathedrals dim
  The birth of Christ is acted o'er;
The kings of Cologne worship him,
  Balthazar, Jasper, Melchior.

The shepherds in the field at night
  Beheld an angel glory-clad,
And shrank away with sore affright.
  "Be not afraid," the angel bade.

"I bring good news to king and clown,
  To you here crouching on the sward;
For there is born in David's town
  A Saviour, which is Christ the Lord.

"Behold the babe is swathed, and laid
  Within a manger." Straight there stood
Beside the angel all arrayed
  A heavenly multitude.

"Glory to God," they sang; "and peace,
  Good pleasure among men."
The wondrous message of release!
  Glory to God again!

Hush! Hark! the waits, far up the street!
  A distant, ghostly charm unfolds,
Of magic music wild and sweet,
  Anomes and clarigolds.

JOHN DAVIDSON.

A CHRISTMAS CAROL

What sweeter music can we bring
Than a carol, for to sing
The birth of this our heavenly King?
Awake the voice! awake the string!
Heart, ear, and eye, and everything!

Dark and dull night, fly hence away,
And give the honour to this day,
That sees December turned to May.

If we may ask the reason, say,
The why and wherefore all things here
Seem like the spring-time of the year?

Why does the chilling winter's morn
Smile, like a field beset with corn?
Or smell, like to a mead new-shorn,
Thus, on the sudden?

                              Come and see
The cause, why things thus fragrant be.
'Tis He is born, whose quickening birth
Gives light and lustre, public mirth,
To heaven, and the under-earth.

We see Him come, and know Him ours,
Who with His sunshine and His showers
Turns all the patient ground to flowers.

The darling of the world is come,
And fit it is we find a room
To welcome Him.   The nobler part
Of all the house here, is the heart,
Which we will give Him; and bequeath
This holly, and this ivy wreath,
To do Him honour; who's our King,
And Lord of all this revelling.

                              ROBERT HERRICK.

A CHILD'S PRESENT TO HIS CHILD-SAVIOUR

Go, pretty child, and bear this flower
Unto thy little Saviour;
And tell Him, by that bud now blown,
He is the Rose of Sharon known;
When thou hast said so, stick it there
Upon his bib, or stomacher;
And tell Him, for good handsel too,
That thou hast brought a whistle new,
Made of a clean straight oaten reed,
To charm his cries at time of need.
Tell Him, for coral thou hast none;
But if thou hadst, He should have one;
But poor thou art, and known to be
Even as moneyless, as He.

          handsel: a gift for good luck.

Lastly, if thou canst win a kiss
From those mellifluous lips of His,
Then never take a second on,
To spoil the first impression.

ROBERT HERRICK.

THE PEACE-GIVER

Thou whose birth on earth
    Angels sang to men,
While thy stars made mirth,
Saviour, at thy birth.
    This day born again;

As this night was bright
    With thy cradle-ray,
Very light of light,
Turn the wild world's night
    To thy perfect day.

Thou the Word and Lord
    In all time and-space
Heard, beheld, adored,
With all ages poured
    Forth before thy face,

Lord, what worth in earth
  Drew thee down to die?
What therein was worth,
Lord, thy death and birth?
  What beneath thy sky?

Thou whose face gives grace
  As the sun's doth heat,
Let thy sunbright face
Lighten time and space
  Here beneath thy feet.

Bid our peace increase,
  Thou that madest morn;
Bid oppression cease;
Bid the night be peace;
  Bid the day be born.

A. C. SWINBURNE.

VARIOUS

TO A SINGER

My soul is an enchanted boat,
  Which, like a sleeping swan, doth float
Upon the silver waves of thy sweet singing;
  And thine doth like an angel sit
  Beside the helm conducting it,
Whilst all the winds with melody are ringing.

It seems to float ever, for ever,
Upon that many-winding river,
Between mountains, woods, abysses,
A paradise of wildernesses!
Till, like one in slumber bound,
Borne to the ocean, I float down, around,
Into a sea profound, of ever-spreading sound.
Meanwhile thy spirit lifts its pinions
In music's most serene dominions;
Catching the winds that fan that happy heaven.
And we sail on, away, afar,
Without a course, without a star,
But by the instinct of sweet music driven;
Till through Elysian garden islets
By thee, most beautiful of pilots,
Where never mortal pinnace glided,
The boat of my desire is guided:
Realms where the air we breathe is love,
Which in the winds on the waves doth move,
Harmonizing this earth with what we feel
above.

P. B. SHELLEY.

THE HAPPY PIPER

Piping down the valleys wild,
  Piping songs of pleasant glee,
On a cloud I saw a child,
  And he laughing said to me:

"Pipe a song about a Lamb!"
  So I piped with merry cheer.
"Piper, pipe that song again";
  So I piped: he wept to hear.

"Drop thy pipe, thy happy pipe;
  Sing thy songs of happy cheer!"
So I sang the same again,
  While he wept with joy to hear.

"Piper, sit thee down and write
  In a book that all may read."
So he vanish'd from my sight,
  And I pluck'd a hollow reed,

And I made a rural pen,
  And I stain'd the water clear,
And I wrote my happy songs
  Every child may joy to hear.

WILLIAM BLAKE.

2

13

1

)

The Destruction of Sennacherib

The Assyrian came down like a wolf on the fold,
And his cohorts were gleaming in purple and
    gold;
And the sheen of their spears was like stars
    on the sea,
When the blue wave rolls nightly on deep
    Galilee.

Like the leaves of the forest when Summer is
    green,
That host with their banners at sunset were
    seen:
Like the leaves of the forest when Autumn hath
    blown,
That host on the morrow lay wither'd and
    strown.

For the Angel of Death spread his wings on
    the blast,
And breathed in the face of the foe as he
    passed;
And the eyes of the sleepers waxed deadly and
    chill,
And their hearts but once heaved, and for ever
    grew still!

And there lay the steed with his nostril all
    wide,
But through it there rolled not the breath of
    his pride:
And the foam of his gasping lay white on the
    turf,
And cold as the spray of the rock-beating
    surf.

And there lay the rider distorted and pale,
With the dew on his brow and the rust on his
    mail;
And the tents were all silent, the banners alone,
The lances unlifted, the trumpet unblown.

And the widows of Ashur are loud in their
    wail,
And the idols are broke in the temple of
    Baal;
And the might of the Gentile, unsmote by
    the sword,
Hath melted like snow in the glance of the
    Lord!

LORD BYRON.

The next two spirited poems—both hailing from America—are inserted with a view to their being useful to boys who have a taste for recitation.

SHERIDAN'S RIDE

Up from the south at break of day,
Bringing to Winchester fresh dismay,
The affrighted air with a shudder bore,
Like a herald in haste, to the chieftain's door,
The terrible grumble and rumble and roar,
Telling the battle was on once more—
And Sheridan twenty miles away!

And wilder still those billows of war
Thundered along the horizon's bar;
And louder yet into Winchester rolled
The roar of that red sea uncontrolled,
Making the blood of the listener cold
As he thought of the stake in that fiery fray,
With Sheridan twenty miles away!

But there is a road from Winchester town,
A good broad highway leading down;
And there, through the flash of the morning
     light,
A steed, as black as the steeds of night,
Was seen to pass as with eagle flight.

6—2

As if he knew the terrible need,
He stretched away with his utmost speed;
Hills rose and fell, but his heart was gay,
With Sheridan fifteen miles away!

Still sprang from those swift hoofs, thundering
    south,
The dust, like the smoke from the cannon's
    mouth,
Or the trail of a comet sweeping faster and faster,
Foreboding to traitors the doom of disaster;
The heart of the steed and the heart of the
    master
Were beating like prisoners assaulting their
    walls,
Impatient to be where the battle-field calls;
Every nerve of the charger was strained to full
    play,
With Sheridan only ten miles away!

The first that the General saw was the groups
Of stragglers, and then—the retreating troops!
What was done—what to do—a glance told
    him both;
And, striking his spurs, with a terrible oath
He dashed down the line 'mid a storm of
    huzzahs,

And the wave of retreat checked its course
    there, because
The sight of the Master compelled it to pause.
With foam and with dust the black charger
    was grey;
By the flash of his eye and his red nostril's play
He seemed to the whole great army to say
"I have brought you Sheridan, all the way
From Winchester town to save the day!"

Hurrah, hurrah, for Sheridan!
Hurrah, hurrah, for horse and man!
And when their statues are placed on high
Under the dome of the Union sky
—The American soldier's Temple of Fame—
There, with the glorious General's name,
Be it said in letters both bold and bright,
"Here is the steed that saved the day
By carrying Sheridan into the fight,
From Winchester—twenty miles away!"

          THOMAS BUCHANAN READ.

COLUMBUS

Behind him lay the gray Azores,
  Behind, the Gates of Hercules;
Before him not the ghost of shores;
  Before him only shoreless seas.
The good mate said: "Now must we pray,
  For lo! the very stars are gone.
Brave Admiral, speak; what shall I say?"
  "Why, say 'Sail on! sail on! and on!'"

"My men grow mutinous day by day;
  My men grow ghastly, wan and weak."
The stout mate thought of home; a spray
  Of salt wave washed his swarthy cheek.
"What shall I say, brave Admiral, say,
  If we sight naught but seas at dawn?"
"Why, you shall say at break of day:
  'Sail on! sail on! sail on! and on!'"

They sailed and sailed, as winds might blow,
  Until at last the blanched mate said:
"Why, now not even God would know
  Should I and all my men fall dead.
These very winds forget their way,
  For God from these dread seas is gone.
Now speak, brave Admiral, speak and say—"
  He said: "Sail on! sail on! and on!"

They sailed. They sailed. Then spake the
    mate:
  "This mad sea shows his teeth to-night!
He curls his lip, he lies in wait,
  He lifts his teeth as if to bite!
Brave Admiral, say but one good word:
  What shall we do when hope is gone?"
The words leapt like a leaping sword:
  "Sail on! sail on! sail on! and on!"

Then, pale and worn, he paced his deck,
  And peered through darkness. Ah, that
    night
Of all dark nights! And then a speck—
  A light! A light! At last a light!
It grew, a starlit flag unfurled!
  It grew to be Time's burst of dawn.
He gained a world; he gave that world
  Its grandest lesson: "On! sail on!"

                       JOAQUIN MILLER.

*Macaulay's " Lays of Ancient Rome," of which this
is the first, deal only with the legends that Rome in her
greatness liked to tell concerning her early beginnings.
Unfortunately there is no similar group of poems treating
of Imperial Rome, the centre of a world-empire ; but
children must please not think of the Mistress of the World
merely as a little riverside town which could free itself
from outside trouble by chopping down a wooden bridge.*

HORATIUS

Lars Porsena of Clusium
   By the Nine Gods he swore
That the great house of Tarquin
   Should suffer wrong no more.
By the Nine Gods he swore it,
   And named a trysting day,
And bade his messengers ride forth
East and west and south and north
   To summon his array.

East and west and south and north
   The messengers ride fast,
And tower and town and cottage
   Have heard the trumpet's blast.
Shame on the false Etruscan
   Who lingers in his home,
When Porsena of Clusium
   Is on the march for Rome.

The horsemen and the footmen
  Are pouring in amain
From many a stately market-place,
  From many a fruitful plain;
From many a lonely hamlet
  Which, hid by beech and pine,
Like an eagle's nest hangs on the crest
  Of purple Apennine;

From lordly Volaterræ,
  Where scowls the far-famed hold
Piled by the hands of giants
  For godlike kings of old;
From sea-girt Populonia
  Whose sentinels descry
Sardinia's snowy mountain-tops
  Fringing the southern sky;

From the proud mart of Pisæ,
  Queen of the western waves,
Where ride Massilia's triremes
  Heavy with fair-haired slaves;
From where sweet Clanis wanders
  Through corn and vines and flowers;
From where Cortona lifts to heaven
  Her diadem of towers.

23

)

Tall are the oaks whose acorns
  Drop in dark Auser's rill;
Fat are the stags that champ the boughs
  Of the Ciminian hill;
Beyond all streams Clitumnus
  Is to the herdsman dear;
Best of all pools the fowler loves
  The great Volsinian mere.

But now no stroke of woodman
  Is heard by Auser's rill;
No hunter tracks the stag's green path
  Up the Ciminian hill;
Unwatched along Clitumnus
  Grazes the milk-white steer;
Unharmed the water-fowl may dip
  In the Volsinian mere.

The harvests of Arretium
  This year old men shall reap;
This year young boys in Umbro
  Shall plunge the struggling sheep;
And in the vats of Luna
  This year the must shall foam
Round the white feet of laughing girls
  Whose sires have marched to Rome.

must : grape-juice.

There be thirty chosén prophets,
  The wisest of the land,
Who alway by Lars Porsena
  Both morn and evening stand:
Evening and morn the Thirty
  Have turned the verses o'er,
Traced from the right on linén white
  By mighty Seers of yore.

And with one voice the Thirty
  Have their glad answer given:
"Go forth, go forth, Lars Porsena;
  Go forth, beloved of Heaven;
Go, and return in glory
  To Clusium's royál dome,
And hang round Nurscia's altars
  The goldén shields of Rome."

And now hath every city
  Sent up her tale of men;
The foot are fourscore thousand,
  The horse are thousands ten.
Before the gates of Sutrium
  Is met the great array.
A proud man was Lars Porsena
  Upon the trysting day!

For all the Etruscan armies
  Were ranged beneath his eye,
And many a banished Roman,
  And many a stout ally;
And with a mighty following
  To join the muster came
The Tusculan Mamilius,
  Prince of the Latian name.

But by the yellow Tiber
  Was tumult and affright:
From all the spacious champaign
  To Rome men took their flight.
A mile around the city
  The throng stopped up the ways;
A fearful sight it was to see,
  Through two long nights and days.

For agèd folk on crutches,
  And women great with child,
And mothers sobbing over babes
  That clung to them and smiled,
And sick men borne in litters
  High on the necks of slaves,
And troops of sun-burned husbandmen
  With reaping-hooks and staves,

And droves of mules and asses
 Laden with skins of wine,
And endless flocks of goats and sheep,
 And endless herds of kine,
And endless trains of waggons
 That creaked beneath the weight
Of corn-sacks and of household goods,
 Choked every roaring gate.

Now from the rock Tarpeian
 Could the wan burghers spy
The line of blazing villages
 Red in the midnight sky.
The Fathers of the City,
 They sat all night and day,
For every hour some horseman came
 With tidings of dismay.

To eastward and to westward
 Have spread the Tuscan bands;
Nor house, nor fence, nor doyecote
 In Crustumerium stands.
Verbenna down to Ostia
 Hath wasted all the plain;
Astur hath stormed Janiculum,
 And the stout guards are slain.

I wis, in all the Senate
  There was no heart so bold
But sore it ached, and fast it beat,
  When that ill news was told.
Forthwith up rose the Consul,
  Up rose the Fathers all;
In haste they girded up their gowns,
  And hied them to the wall.

They held a council standing
  Before the River-Gate;
Short time was there, ye well may guess,
  For musing or debate.
Out spake the Consul roundly:
  "The bridge must straight go down;
For, since Janiculum is lost,
  Nought else can save the town."

Just then a scout came flying,
  All wild with haste and fear:
"To arms! to arms! Sir Consul:
  Lars Porsena is here."
On the low hills to westward
  The Consul fixed his eye,
And saw the swarthy storm of dust
  Rise fast along the sky.

And nearer fast and nearer
  Doth the red whirlwind come;
And louder still and still more loud
From underneath that rolling cloud
Is heard the trumpet's war-note proud,
  The trampling, and the hum.
And plainly and more plainly
  Now through the gloom appears,
Far to left and far to right,
In broken gleams of dark-blue light,
The long array of helmets bright,
  The long array of spears.

And plainly and more plainly
  Above that glimmering line
Now might ye see the banners
  Of twelve fair cities shine;
But the banner of proud Clusium
  Was highest of them all,
The terror of the Umbrian,
The terror of the Gaul.

And plainly and more plainly
  Now might the burghers know,
By port and vest, by horse and crest,
  Each warlike Lucumo.

Lucumo : Etruscan nobleman.

There Cilnius of Arretium
  On his fleet roan was seen;
And Astur of the fourfold shield,
Girt with the brand none else may wield,
Tolumnius with the belt of gold,
And dark Verbenna from the hold
  By reedy Thrasymene.

Fast by the royal standard
  O'erlooking all the war,
Lars Porsena of Clusium
  Sate in his ivory car.
By the right wheel rode Mamilius,
  Prince of the Latian name;
And by the left false Sextus,
  That wrought the deed of shame.

But when the face of Sextus
  Was seen among the foes,
A yell that rent the firmament
  From all the town arose.
On the house-tops was no woman
  But spat towards him, and hissed;
No child but screamed out curses,
  And shook its little fist.

But the Consul's brow was sad,
  And the Consul's speech was low,
And darkly looked he at the wall,
  And darkly at the foe.
"Their van will be upon us
  Before the bridge goes down;
And if they once may win the bridge,
  What hope to save the town?"

Then out spake brave Horatius,
  The Captain of the gate:
"To every man upon this earth
  Death cometh soon or late;
And how can man die better
  Than facing fearful odds
For the ashes of his fathers
  And the temples of his Gods,

And for the tender mother
  Who dandled him to rest,
And for the wife who nurses
  His baby at her breast,
And for the holy maidens
  Who feed the eternal flame,
To save them from false Sextus
  That wrought the deed of shame?

Hew down the bridge, Sir Consul,
    With all the speed ye may;
I, with two more to help me,
    Will hold the foe in play.
In yon strait path a thousand
    May well be stopped by three:
Now who will stand on either hand,
    And keep the bridge with me?"

Then out spake Spurius Lartius,
    A Ramnian proud was he:
"Lo, I will stand at thy right hand,
    And keep the bridge with thee."
And out spake strong Herminius,
    Of Titian blood was he:
"I will abide on thy left side,
    And keep the bridge with thee."

"Horatius," quoth the Consul,
    "As thou sayest, so let it be."
And straight against that great array
    Forth went the dauntless Three.
For Romans in Rome's quarrel
    Spared neither land nor gold,
Nor son nor wife, nor limb nor life
    In the brave days of old.

Then none was for a party;
  Then all were for the State;
Then the great man helped the poor,
  And the poor man loved the great;
Then lands were fairly portioned;
  Then spoils were fairly sold;
The Romans were like brothers
  In the brave days of old.

Now Roman is to Roman
  More hateful than a foe,
And the Tribunes beard the high,
  And the Fathers grind the low.
As we wax hot in faction,
  In battle we wax cold:
Wherefore men fight not as they fought
  In the brave days of old.

Now while the Three were tightening
  Their harness on their backs,
The Consul was the foremost man
  To take in hand an axe:
And Fathers mixed with Commons
  Seized hatchet, bar, and crow,
And smote upon the planks above,
  And loosed the props below.

7—2

Meanwhile the Tuscan army,
  Right glorious to behold,
Came flashing back the noonday light,
Rank behind rank, like surges bright
  Of a broad sea of gold.
Four hundred trumpets sounded
  A peal of warlike glee,
As that great host, with measured tread,
And spears advanced, and ensigns spread,
Rolled slowly towards the bridge's head,
  Where stood the dauntless Three.

The Three stood calm and silent,
  And looked upon the foes,
And a great shout of laughter
  From all the vanguard rose:
And forth three chiefs came spurring
  Before that deep array;
To earth they sprang, their swords they drew,
And lifted high their shields, and flew
  To win the narrow way;

Aunus from green Tifernum,
  Lord of the Hill of Vines;
And Seius, whose eight hundred slaves
  Sicken in Ilva's mines;

And Picus, long to Clusium
    Vassal in peace and war,
Who led to fight his Umbrian powers
From that grey crag where, girt with towers,
The fortress of Nequinum lowers
    O'er the pale waves of Nar.

Stout Lartius hurled down Aunus
    Into the stream beneath:
Herminius struck at Seius,
    And clove him to the teeth:
At Picus brave Horatius
    Darted one fiery thrust,
And the proud Umbrian's gilded arms
    Clashed in the bloody dust.

Then Ocnus of Falerii
    Rushed on the Roman Three;
And Lausulus of Urgo,
    The rover of the sea;
And Aruns of Volsinium,
    Who slew the great wild boar,
The great wild boar that had his den
Amidst the reeds of Cosa's fen,
And wasted fields, and slaughtered men,
    Along Albinia's shore.

Herminius smote down Aruns:
  Lartius laid Ocnus low:
Right to the heart of Lausulus
  Horatius sent a blow.
"Lie there," he cried, "fell pirate!
  No more, aghast and pale,
From Ostia's walls the crowd shall mark
The track of thy destroying bark.
No more Campania's hinds shall fly
To woods and caverns when they spy
  Thy thrice-accursed sail."

But now no sound of laughter
  Was heard amongst the foes.
A wild and wrathful clamour
  From all the vanguard rose.
Six spears' lengths from the entrance
  Halted that deep array,
And for a space no man came forth
  To win the narrow way.

But hark! the cry is "Astur!"
  And lo! the ranks divide;
And the great Lord of Luna
  Comes with his stately stride.
Upon his ample shoulders
  Clangs loud the fourfold shield,

And in his hand he shakes the brand
  Which none but he can wield.

He smiled on those bold Romans
  A smile serene and high;
He eyed the flinching Tuscans,
  And scorn was in his eye.
Quoth he, "The she-wolf's litter
  Stand savagely at bay:
But will ye dare to follow,
  If Astúr clears the way?"

Then, whirling up his broadsword
  With both hands to the height,
He rushed against Horatius,
  And smote with all his might.
With shield and blade Horatius
  Right deftly turned the blow:
The blow, though turned, came yet too nigh;
It missed his helm, but gashed his thigh:
The Tuscans raised a joyful cry
  To see the red blood flow.

He reeled, and on Herminius
  He leaned one breathing-space;
Then, like a wild cat mad with wounds,
  Sprang right at Astúr's face.

Through teeth, and skull, and helmet,
　So fierce a thrust he sped
The good sword stood a handbreadth out
　Behind the Tuscan's head.

And the great Lord of Luna
　Fell at that deadly stroke,
As falls on Mount Alvernus
　A thunder-smitten oak:
Far o'er the crashing forest
　The giant arms lie spread;
And the pale augurs, muttering low,
　Gaze on the blasted head.

On Astur's throat Horatius
　Right firmly pressed his heel,
And thrice and four times tugged amain,
　Ere he wrenched out the steel.
"And see," he cried, "the welcome,
　Fair guests, that waits you here!
What noble Lucumo comes next
　To taste our Roman cheer?"

But at his haughty challenge
　A sullen murmur ran,
Mingled of wrath and shame and dread,
　Along that glittering van.

There lacked not men of prowess,
  Nor men of lordly race;
For all Etruria's noblest
  Were round the fatal place.

But all Etruria's noblest
  Felt their hearts sink to see
On the earth the bloody corpses,
  In the path the dauntless Three:
And, from the ghastly entrance
  Where those bold Romans stood,
All shrank, like boys who unaware,
Ranging the woods to start a hare,
Come to the mouth of the dark lair
Where, growling low, a fierce old bear
  Lies amidst bones and blood.

Was none who would be foremost
  To lead such dire attack;
But those behind cried "Forward!"
  And those before cried "Back!"
And backward now and forward
  Wavers the deep array;
And on the tossing sea of steel,
To and fro the standards reel;
And the victorious trumpet-peal
  Dies fitfully away.

Yet one man for one moment
   Strode out before the crowd;
Well known was he to all the Three,
   And they gave him greeting loud.
"Now welcome, welcome, Sextus!
   Now welcome to thy home!
Why dost thou stay, and turn away?
   Here lies the road to Rome."

Thrice looked he at the city;
   Thrice looked he at the dead;
And thrice came on in fury,
   And thrice turned back in dread:
And, white with fear and hatred,
   Scowled at the narrow way
Where, wallowing in a pool of blood,
   The bravest Tuscans lay.

But meanwhile axe and lever
   Have manfully been plied;
And now the bridge hangs tottering
   Above the boiling tide.
"Come back, come back, Horatius!"
   Loud cried the Fathers all.
"Back, Lartius! back, Herminius!
   Back, ere the ruin fall!"

Back darted Spurius Lartius;
  Herminius darted back:
And, as they passed, beneath their feet
  They felt the timbers crack.
But, when they turned their faces,
  And on the farther shore
Saw brave Horatius stand alone,
  They would have crossed once more.

But with a crash like thunder
  Fell every loosened beam,
And, like a dam the mighty wreck
  Lay right athwart the stream:
And a long shout of triumph
  Rose from the walls of Rome,
As to the highest turret-tops
  Was splashed the yellow foam.

And, like a horse unbroken
  When first he feels the rein,
The furious river struggled hard,
  And tossed his tawny mane;
And burst the curb, and bounded,
  Rejoicing to be free;
And whirling down, in fierce career,
Battlement, and plank, and pier,
  Rushed headlong to the sea.

Alone stood brave Horatius,
  But constant still in mind;
Thrice thirty thousand foes before,
  And the broad flood behind.
"Down with him!" cried false Sextus,
  With a smile on his pale face.
"Now yield thee," cried Lars Porsena,
  "Now yield thee to our grace."

Round turned he, as not deigning
  Those craven ranks to see;
Nought spake he to Lars Porsena,
  To Sextus nought spake he;
But he saw on Palatinus
  The white porch of his home;
And he spake to the noble river
  That rolls by the towers of Rome.

"O Tiber! father Tiber!
  To whom the Romans pray,
A Roman's life, a Roman's arms
  Take thou in charge this day!"
So he spake, and speaking sheathèd
  The good sword by his side,
And with his harness on his back
  Plunged headlong in the tide.

No sound of joy or sorrow
  Was heard from either bank;
But friends and foes in dumb surprise,
With parted lips and straining eyes,
  Stood gazing where he sank; .
And when above the surges
  They saw his crest appear,
All Rome sent forth a rapturous cry,
And even the ranks of Tuscany
  Could scarce forbear to cheer.

But fiercely ran the current,
  Swollen high by months of rain:
And fast his blood was flowing;
  And he was sore in pain,
And heavy with his armour,
  And spent with changing blows:
And oft they thought him sinking,
  But still again he rose.

Never, I ween, did swimmer,
  In such an evil case,
Struggle through such a raging flood
  Safe to the landing-place:
But his limbs were borne-up bravely
  By the brave heart within,

And our good father Tiber
  Bare bravely up his chin.

"Curse on him!" quoth false Sextus;
  "Will not the villain drown?
But for this stay ere close of day
  We should have sacked the town!"
"Heaven help him!" quoth Lars Porsena,
  "And bring him safe to shore;
For such a gallant feat of arms
  Was never seen before."

And now he feels the bottom;
  Now on dry earth he stands;
Now round him throng the Fathers
  To press his gory hands;
And now with shouts and clapping,
  And noise of weeping loud,
He enters through the River-Gate,
  Borne by the joyous crowd.

They gave him of the corn-land,
  That was of public right,
As much as two strong oxen
  Could plough from morn till night;

And they made a molten image,
  And set it up on high,
And there it stands unto this day
  To witness if I lie.

It stands in the Comitium
  Plain for all folk to see;
Horatius in his harness,
  Halting upon one knee:
And underneath is written,
  In letters all of gold,
How valiantly he kept the bridge
  In the brave days of old.

And still his name sounds stirring
  Unto the men of Rome,
As the trumpet-blast that cries to them
  To charge the Volscian home;
And wives still pray to Juno
  For boys with hearts as bold
As his who kept the bridge so well
  In the brave days of old.

And in the nights of winter,
  When the cold north winds blow,
And the long howling of the wolves
  Is heard amidst the snow;

When round the lonely cottage
  Roars loud the tempest's din,
And the good logs of Algidus
  Roar louder yet within;

When the oldest cask is opened,
  And the largest lamp is lit;
When the chestnuts glow in the embers,
  And the kid turns on the spit;
When young and old in circle
  Around the firebrands close;
When the girls are weaving baskets,
  And the lads are shaping bows;

When the goodman mends his armour
  And trims his helmet's plume;
When the goodwife's shuttle merrily
  Goes flashing through the loom;
With weeping and with laughter
  Still is the story told,
How well Horatius kept the bridge
  In the brave days of old.

LORD MACAULAY.

23 /
11
15
19
18.
17
14
20   *2.16*
18   *4.14*
13   *4 21*
16   *4 10*
17   *2 23*
9   *0 7*
17
23   *58*
9

INDEX OF AUTHORS

G.   8

INDEX OF FIRST LINES

Cambridge:
PRINTED BY JOHN CLAY, M.A.
AT THE UNIVERSITY PRESS

The Cambridge Book
of
Poetry for Children

PART II

CAMBRIDGE UNIVERSITY PRESS
C. F. CLAY, Manager
London: FETTER LANE, E.C.
Edinburgh: 100 PRINCES STREET

Bombay, Calcutta and Madras: MACMILLAN AND CO., Ltd.
Toronto: J. M. DENT AND SONS, Ltd.
Tokyo: THE MARUZEN-KABUSHIKI-KAISHA

Copyrighted in the United States of America by
G. P. PUTNAM'S SONS,
2, 4 AND 6, WEST 45TH STREET, NEW YORK CITY

The Cambridge Book

of

Poetry for Children

Edited by

KENNETH GRAHAME

Author of *The Golden Age, Dream Days, The Wind
in the Willows, etc.*

PART II

Cambridge:
at the University Press
1916

NOTE

The Editor has to express his thanks for permission to use copyright matter to the Editor of *A Sailor's Garland* and its publishers, Messrs Methuen, to Mr Elkin Mathews for the poem by Richard Hovey, to Messrs G. Routledge & Sons for a poem by Joaquin Miller.

CONTENTS

NATURE, COUNTRY AND THE OPEN AIR

GREEN SEAS AND SAILOR MEN

Contents

1 5 1 5 = 18   = 1 t 5 m
.25 28 14 15   93   first page

l   )

NATURE, COUNTRY, AND THE OPEN AIR

To Meadows

Ye have been fresh and green,
  Ye have been fill'd with flowers;
And ye the walks have been
  Where maids have spent their hours.
You have beheld how they
  With wicker arks did come
To kiss and bear away
  The richer cowslips home.
You've heard them sweetly sing,
  And seen them in a round:
Each virgin like a spring,
  With honeysuckles crown'd.

But now we see none here
  Whose silv'ry feet did tread
And with dishevelled hair
  Adorn'd this smoother mead.
Like unthrifts, having spent
  Your stock, and needy grown,
You're left here to lament
  Your poor estates, alone.

ROBERT HERRICK.

THE BROOK

I come from haunts of coot and hern,
   I make a sudden sally,
And sparkle out among the fern,
   To bicker down a valley.

By thirty hills I hurry down,
   Or slip between the ridges,
By twenty thorps, a little town,
   And half a hundred bridges.

I chatter over stony ways
   In little sharps and trebles,
I bubble into eddying bays,
   I babble on the pebbles.

With many a curve my banks I fret
   By many a field and fallow,
And many a fairy foreland set
   With willow-weed and mallow.

I chatter, chatter, as I flow
   To join the brimming river,
For men may come and men may go,
   But I go on for ever.

hern : heron.   *thorps :* villages.

I wind about and in and out,
  With here a blossom sailing,
And here and there a lusty trout,
  And here and there a grayling.

And here and there a foamy flake
  Upon me, as I travel
With many a silvery waterbreak
  Above the golden gravel.

I steal by lawns and grassy plots,
  I slide by hazel covers;
I move the sweet forget-me-nots
  That grow for happy lovers.

I slip, I slide, I gloom, I glance,
  Among my skimming swallows;
I make the netted sunbeam dance
  Against my sandy shallows.

I murmur under moon and stars
  In brambly wildernesses;
I linger by my shingly bars;
  I loiter round my cresses;

And out again I curve and flow
  To join the brimming river,
For men may come and men may go,
  But I go on for ever.

ALFRED, LORD TENNYSON.

1—2

William Wordsworth

RECOLLECTIONS OF EARLY CHILDHOOD

There was a time when meadow, grove, and
      stream,
  The earth, and every common sight,
    To me did seem
    Apparell'd in celestial light,
The glory and the freshness of a dream.
It is not now as it hath been of yore;—
    Turn wheresoe'er I may,
        By night or day,
The things which I have seen I now can see no
      more.

    The rainbow comes and goes,
    And lovely is the rose;
    The moon doth with delight
Look round her when the heavens are bare;
      Waters on a starry night
    Are beautiful and fair;
    The sunshine is a glorious birth;
    But yet I know, where'er I go,
That there hath passed away a glory from the
      earth.

Now, while the birds thus sing a joyous song,
  And while the young lambs bound
  As to the tabor's sound,

To me alone there came a thought of grief:
A timely utterance gave that thought relief,
    And I again am strong.
The cataracts blow their trumpets from the
    steep;
  No more shall grief of mine the season wrong;
  I hear the echoes through the mountains
    throng,
The winds come to me from the fields of sleep,
    And all the earth is gay;
      Land and sea
  Give themselves up to jollity,
    And with the heart of May
  Doth every beast keep holiday;—
      Thou Child of Joy,
Shout round me, let me hear thy shouts, thou
    happy Shepherd-boy!

Ye blessed creatures, I have heard the call
  Ye to each other make; I see
The heavens laugh with you in your jubilee;
  My heart is at your festival,
  My head hath its coronal,
The fulness of your bliss, I feel—I feel it all.
    O evil day! if I were sullen
      While Earth herself is adorning,
      This sweet May morning,

And the children are culling
    On every side,
In a thousand valleys far and wide,

Fresh flowers; while the sun shines warm,
And the babe leaps up on his mother's arm:—
    I hear, I hear, with joy I hear!
    —But there's a tree, of many one,
A single field which I have look'd upon,
Both of them speak of something that is gone:
    The pansy at my feet
    Doth the same tale repeat:
Whither is fled the visionary gleam?
Where is it now, the glory and the dream?

Our birth is but a sleep and a forgetting:
The Soul that rises with us, our life's Star,
    Hath had elsewhere its setting,
        And cometh from afar:
    Not in entire forgetfulness,
    And not in utter nakedness,
But trailing clouds of glory do we come
    From God, who is our home:
Heaven lies about us in our infancy!
Shades of the prison-house begin to close
    Upon the growing Boy,
But he beholds the light, and whence it flows,

He sees it in his joy;
The Youth, who daily further from the east
  Must travel, still is Nature's priest,
    And by the vision splendid
    Is on his way attended;
At length the man perceives it die away,
And fade into the light of common day.

·   ·   ·   ·   ·   ·

WILLIAM WORDSWORTH.

*(This is only a portion of the poem, which later you
should take an opportunity of reading as a whole.)*

TO AUTUMN

Season of mists and mellow fruitfulness!
  Close bosom-friend of the maturing sun;
Conspiring with him how to load and bless
  With fruit the vines that round the thatch-
      eaves run;
To bend with apples the moss'd cottage-trees,
And fill all fruit with ripeness to the core;
  To swell the gourd, and plump the hazel
      shells
With a sweet kernel; to set budding more,
And still more, later flowers for the bees,
Until they think warm days will never cease,
  For Summer has o'er-brimm'd their clammy
      cells.

Who hath not seen Thee oft amid thy store?
  Sometimes whoever seeks abroad may find
Thee sitting careless on a granary floor,
  Thy hair soft-lifted by the winnowing wind;
Or on a half-reap'd furrow sound asleep,
  Drowsed with the fume of poppies, while
    thy hook
    Spares the next swath and all its twinèd
    flowers;
And sometimes like a gleaner thou dost keep
  Steady thy laden head across a brook;
  Or by a cider-press, with patient look,
    Thou watchest the last oozings hours by
    hours.

Where are the songs of Spring? Ay, where
    are they?
  Think not of them, thou hast thy music too,—
While barrèd clouds bloom the soft-dying
    day,
  And touch the stubble-plains with rosy hue;
Then in a wailful choir the small gnats mourn
  Among the river sallows, borne aloft
    Or sinking as the light wind lives or dies;
And full-grown lambs loud bleat from hilly
    bourn;

sallows: willows.   *bourn:* stream, water-course.

Hedge-crickets sing; and now with treble
soft
The redbreast whistles from a garden-
croft;
And gathering swallows twitter in the
skies.

JOHN KEATS.

ODE TO THE WEST WIND

I.

O wild West Wind, thou breath of Autumn's
being,
Thou from whose unseen presence the leaves
dead
Are driven, like ghosts from an enchanter
fleeing,

Yellow, and black, and pale, and hectic red,
Pestilence-stricken multitudes! O thou
Who chariotest to their dark wintry bed

The wingèd seeds, where they lie cold and
low,
Each like a corpse within its grave, until
Thine azure sister of the Spring shall blow

croft : enclosure.

Her clarion o'er the dreaming earth, and fill
  (Driving sweet buds like flocks to feed in air)
With living hues and odours plain and hill:

Wild Spirit, which art moving everywhere;
Destroyer and preserver; hear, O hear!

II.

Thou on whose stream, 'mid the steep sky's
    commotion,
  Loose clouds like earth's decaying leaves
    are shed,
Shook from the tangled boughs of heaven and
    ocean,
  Angels of rain and lightning! there are
    spread
On the blue surface of thine airy surge,
  Like the bright hair uplifted from the head
Of some fierce Maenad, even from the dim
    verge
  Of the horizon to the zenith's height,
The locks of the approaching storm. Thou dirge

  Of the dying year, to which this closing night
Will be the dome of a vast sepulchre,
  Vaulted with all thy congregated might

Maenad . a priestess of Bacchus, the wine-god.

Of vapours, from whose solid atmosphere
Black rain, and fire, and hail, will burst : O hear!

III.

Thou who didst waken from his summer dreams
  The blue Mediterranean, where he lay,
Lull'd by the coil of his crystalline streams,

    Beside a pumice isle in Baiae's bay,
And saw in sleep old palaces and towers
  Quivering within the wave's intenser day,

All overgrown with azure moss, and flowers
  So sweet, the sense faints picturing them!
    Thou
For whose path the Atlantic's level powers

  Cleave themselves into chasms, while far
    below
The sea-blooms and the oozy woods which wear
  The sapless foliage of the ocean, know

Thy voice, and suddenly grow grey with fear,
And tremble and despoil themselves : O hear!

IV.

If I were a dead leaf thou mightest bear;
  If I were a swift cloud to fly with thee;
A wave to pant beneath thy power, and share

    coil : confused noise, murmur.   *pumice :* formed of volcanic
lava.

The impulse of thy strength, only less free
Than thou, O uncontrollable! if even
  I were as in my boyhood, and could be

The comrade of thy wanderings over heaven,
  As then, when to outstrip thy skiey speed
Scarce seem'd a vision—I would ne'er have
    striven

  As thus with thee in prayer in my sore need.
O! lift me as a wave, a leaf, a cloud!
  I fall upon the thorns of life! I bleed!

A heavy weight of years has chain'd and bow'd
One too like thee—tameless, and swift, and
    proud.

V.

Make me thy lyre, even as the forest is:
  What if my leaves are falling like its own?
The tumult of thy mighty harmonies

  Will take from both a deep autumnal tone,
Sweet though in sadness. Be thou, Spirit
    fierce,
  My spirit! Be thou me, impetuous one!

Drive my dead thoughts over the universe,
  Like wither'd leaves, to quicken a new birth;
And, by the incantation of this verse,

Scatter, as from an unextinguish'd hearth
Ashes and sparks, my words among mankind!
Be through my lips to unawaken'd earth

The trumpet of a prophecy! O Wind,
If Winter comes, can Spring be far behind?

PERCY BYSSHE SHELLEY.

TO A SKYLARK

Hail to thee, blithe spirit!
Bird thou never wert—
That from heaven or near it
Pourest thy full heart
In profuse strains of unpremeditated art.

Higher still and higher
From the earth thou springest
Like a cloud of fire;
The blue deep thou wingest,
And singing still dost soar, and soaring ever
singest.

In the golden lightning
Of the sunken sun,
O'er which clouds are bright'ning,
Thou dost float and run,
Like an unbodied joy whose race is just begun.

The pale purple even
  Melts around thy flight;
Like a star of heaven,
  In the broad daylight
Thou art unseen, but yet I hear thy shrill
  delight.

Keen as are the arrows
  Of that silver sphere,
Whose intense lamp narrows
  In the white dawn clear,
Until we hardly see, we feel that it is there.

All the earth and air
  With thy voice is loud,
As, when night is bare,
  From one lonely cloud
The moon rains out her beams, and heaven is
  overflow'd.

What thou art we know not;
  What is most like thee?
From rainbow clouds there flow not
  Drops so bright to see,
As from thy presence showers a rain of
  melody:—

Like a poet hidden
In the light of thought,
Singing hymns unbidden,
Till the world is wrought
To sympathy with hopes and fears it heeded
not:

Like a high-born maiden
In a palace tower,
Soothing her love-laden
Soul in secret hour
With music sweet as love, which overflows her
bower:

Like a glow-worm golden
In a dell of dew,
Scattering unbeholden
Its aërial hue
Among the flowers and grass which screen it
from the view:

Like a rose embower'd
In its own green leaves,
By warm winds deflower'd,
Till the scent it gives
Makes faint with too much sweet these heavy-
wingèd thieves:

Sound of vernal showers
   On the twinkling grass,
Rain-awaken'd flowers—
   All that ever was
Joyous and clear and fresh—thy music doth
   surpass.

   Teach us, sprite or bird,
     What sweet thoughts are thine:
   I have never heard
     Praise of love or wine
That panted forth a flood of rapture so divine.

   Chorus hymeneal
     Or triumphal chant,
Match'd with thine would be all
     But an empty vaunt—
A thing wherein we feel there is some hidden
   want.

   What objects are the fountains
     Of thy happy strain?
   What fields, or waves, or mountains?
     What shapes of sky or plain?
What love of thine own kind? what ignorance
   of pain?

With thy clear keen joyance
　Languor cannot be:
Shadow of annoyance
　Never came near thee:
Thou lovest, but ne'er knew love's sad satiety.

Waking or asleep,
　Thou of death must deem
Things more true and deep
　Than we mortals dream,
Or how could thy notes flow in such a crystal
　stream?

We look before and after,
　And pine for what is not:
Our sincerest laughter
　With some pain is fraught;
Our sweetest songs are those that tell of saddest
　thought.

Yet if we could scorn
　Hate and pride and fear,
If we were things born
　Not to shed a tear,
I know not how thy joy we ever should come
　near.

Better than all measures
 Of delightful sound,
Better than all treasures
 That in books are found,
Thy skill to poet were, thou scorner of the
 ground!
  Teach me half the gladness
   That thy brain must know;
  Such harmonious madness
   From my lips would flow,
The world should listen then, as I am listening
 now.   PERCY BYSSHE SHELLEY.

THE MOON-GODDESS
 Queen and huntress, chaste and fair,
  Now the sun is laid to sleep,
 Seated in thy silver chair,
  State in wonted manner keep:
   Hesperus entreats thy light,
   Goddess excellently bright.

 Earth, let not thy envious shade
  Dare itself to interpose;
 Cynthia's shining orb was made
  Heaven to clear when day did close:
   Bless us then with wishèd sight,
   Goddess excellently bright.

Lay thy bow of pearl apart,
  And thy crystal-shining quiver;
Give unto the flying hart
  Space to breathe, how short soever:
    Thou that mak'st a day of night—
    Goddess excellently bright.

                Ben Jonson.

HOME-THOUGHTS FROM ABROAD

O, to be in England
Now that April's there,
And whoever wakes in England
Sees, some morning, unaware,
That the lowest boughs and the brushwood sheaf
Round the elm-tree bole are in tiny leaf,
While the chaffinch sings on the orchard bough
In England—now!

And after April, when May follows,
And the white throat builds, and all the swallows!
Hark, where my blossom'd pear-tree in the
    hedge
Leans to the field and scatters on the clover
Blossoms and dewdrops—at the bent spray's
    edge—
That's the wise thrush; he sings each song
    twice over,

2—2

Lest you should think he never could recapture
The first fine careless rapture!
And though the fields look rough with hoary
        dew,
All will be gay when noontide wakes anew
The buttercups, the little children's dower
—Far brighter than this gaudy melon-flower!

ROBERT BROWNING.

HOME-THOUGHTS FROM THE SEA

Nobly, nobly Cape Saint Vincent to the North-
        west died away;
Sunset ran, one glorious blood-red, reeking
        into Cadiz Bay;
Bluish 'mid the burning water, full in face
        Trafalgar lay;
In the dimmest North-east distance dawn'd
        Gibraltar grand and gray;
"Here and here did England help me: how
        can I help England?"—say,
Whoso turns as I, this evening, turn to God to
        praise and pray,
While Jove's planet rises yonder, silent over
        Africa.

ROBERT BROWNING.

GREEN SEAS AND SAILOR MEN

1. *The Call of the Sea*

YE MARINERS OF ENGLAND

Ye Mariners of England!
    That guard our native seas;
Whose flag has braved a thousand years
    The battle and the breeze!
Your glorious standard launch again
    To match another foe;
And sweep through the deep,
    While the stormy winds do blow!
While the battle rages loud and long,
    And the stormy winds do blow.

The spirits of your fathers
    Shall start from every wave;
For the deck it was their field of fame,
    And Ocean was their grave:
Where Blake and mighty Nelson fell
    Your manly hearts shall glow,
As ye sweep through the deep,
    While the stormy winds do blow!
While the battle rages loud and long,
    And the stormy winds do blow.

Britannia needs no bulwarks,
　　No towers along the steep;
Her march is o'er the mountain-waves,
　　Her home is on the deep.
With thunders from her native oak
　　She quells the floods below,
As they roar on the shore,
　　When the stormy winds do blow!
When the battle rages loud and long,
　　And the stormy winds do blow.

The meteor flag of England
　　Shall yet terrific burn;
Till danger's troubled night depart
　　And the star of peace return!
Then, then, ye ocean-warriors!
　　Our song and feast shall flow
To the fame of your name,
　　When the storm has ceased to blow!
When the fiery fight is heard no more,
　　And the storm has ceased to blow.

THOMAS CAMPBELL.

THE SECRET OF THE SEA

　　Ah! what pleasant visions haunt me
　　　　As I gaze upon the sea!
　　All the old romantic legends,
　　　　All my dreams come back to me.

Sails of silk and ropes of sendal,
  Such as gleam in ancient lore;
And the singing of the sailors,
  And the answer from the shore!

Most of all, the Spanish ballad
  Haunts me oft, and tarries long,
Of the noble Count Arnaldos
  And the sailor's mystic song.

Telling how the Count Arnaldos,
  With his hawk upon his hand,
Saw a fair and stately galley,
  Steering onward to the land;—

How he heard the ancient helmsman
  Chant a song so wild and clear,
That the sailing sea-bird slowly
  Poised upon the mast to hear,

Till his soul was full of longing,
  And he cried, with impulse strong,—
"Helmsman! for the love of heaven,
  Teach me, too, that wondrous song!"

"Wouldst   thou," — so   the   helmsman
      answered,
  "Learn the secret of the sea?
Only those who brave its dangers
  Comprehend its mystery!"

sendal : coarse narrow silken material.

In each sail that skims the horizon,
  In each landward-blowing breeze,
I behold that stately galley,
  Hear those mournful melodies.

Till my soul is full of longing
  For the secret of the sea,
And the heart of the great ocean
  Sends a thrilling pulse through me.

            H. W. LONGFELLOW.

A DUTCH PICTURE

Simon Danz has come home again,
  From cruising about with his buccaneers;
He has singed the beard of the King of Spain,
And carried away the Dean of Jaen,
  And sold him in Algiers.

In his house by the Maese, with its roof of tiles,
  And weathercocks flying aloft in air,
There are silver tankards in antique styles,
Plunder of convent and castle, and piles
  Of carpets rich and rare.

In his tulip-garden there by the town,
  Overlooking the sluggish stream,
With his Moorish cap and dressing-gown,
The old sea-captain, hale and brown,
  Walks in a waking dream.

      buccaneers : sea rovers, pirates.

A smile in his gray mustachio lurks
   Whenever he thinks of the King of Spain,
And the listed tulips look like Turks,
And the silent gardener as he works
   Is changed to the Dean of Jaen.

The windmills on the outermost
   Verge of the landscape in the haze,
To him are towers on the Spanish coast,
With whiskered sentinels at their post,
   Though this is the river Maese.

But when the winter rains begin,
   He sits and smokes by the blazing brands,
And old seafaring men come in,
Goat-bearded, gray, and with double chin,
   And rings upon their hands.

They sit there in the shadow and shine
   Of the flickering fire of the winter night;
Figures in colour and design
Like those by Rembrandt of the Rhine,
   Half darkness and half light.

And they talk of ventures lost or won,
   And their talk is ever and ever the same,
While they drink the red wine of Tarragon,
From the cellars of some Spanish Don,
   Or convent set on flame.

      listed : striped   *Jaen.* a town in Spain.

Restless at times, with heavy strides
  He paces his parlour to and fro;
He is like a ship that at anchor rides,
And swings with the rising and falling tides,
  And tugs at her anchor-tow.

Voices mysterious far and near,
  Sound of the wind and sound of the sea,
Are calling and whispering in his ear,
"Simon Danz! Why stayest thou here?
  Come forth and follow me!"

So he thinks he shall take to the sea again
  For one more cruise with his buccaneers,
To singe the beard of the King of Spain,
And capture another Dean of Jaen,
  And sell him in Algiers.

                  H. W. LONGFELLOW.

SEA MEMORIES

Often I think of the beautiful town
  That is seated by the sea;
Often in thought go up and down
The pleasant streets of that dear old town,
  And my youth comes back to me.
    And a verse of a Lapland song
    Is haunting my memory still:
    "A boy's will is the wind's will,
And the thoughts of youth are long, long
    thoughts."

I can see the shadowy lines of its trees,
  And catch, in sudden gleams,
The sheen of the far-surrounding seas,
And islands that were the Hesperides
  Of all my boyish dreams.
    And the burden of that old song,
    It murmurs and whispers still:
    "A boy's will is the wind's will,
And the thoughts of youth are long, long
      thoughts."
I remember the black wharves and the slips,
  And the sea-tides tossing free;
And the Spanish sailors with bearded lips,
And the beauty and mystery of the ships,
  And the magic of the sea.
    And the voice of that wayward song
    Is singing and saying still:
    "A boy's will is the wind's will,
And the thoughts of youth are long, long
      thoughts."   H. W. LONGFELLOW.

THE SEA GYPSY

    I am fever'd with the sunset,
    I am fretful with the bay,
    For the wander-thirst is on me
    And my soul is in Cathay.

Hesperides: the fabulous "Isles of the Blest" in far western seas.

There's a schooner in the offing,
With her topsails shot with fire,
And my heart has gone aboard her
For the Islands of Desire.

I must forth again to-morrow!
With the sunset I must be
Hull down on the trail of rapture
In the wonder of the Sea.

RICHARD HOVEY.

THE GREENWICH PENSIONER

'Twas in the good ship *Rover*,
   I sailed the world all round,
And for three years and over
   I ne'er touched British ground;
At length in England landed,
   I left the roaring main,
Found all relations stranded,
      And went to sea again,
      And went to sea again.

That time bound straight for Portugal,
   Right fore and aft we bore,
But when we made Cape Ortegal,
   A gale blew off the shore;

She lay, so did it shock her,
  A log upon the main,
Till, saved from Davy's locker,
    We put to sea again,
    We put to sea again.

Next sailing in a frigate
  I got my timber toe.
I never more shall jig it
  As once I used to do;
My leg was shot off fairly,
  All by a ship of Spain;
But I could swab the galley,
    I went to sea, again,
    I went to sea again.

And still I am enabled
  To bring up in the rear,
Although I'm quite disabled
  And lie in Greenwich tier.
There's schooners in the river
  A riding to the chain,
But I shall never, ever
    Put out to sea again,
    Put out to sea again.

      From *A Sailor's Garland.*

THE PRESS-GANG

> Here's the tender coming,
>> Pressing all the men;
>>> O, dear honey,
>> What shall we do then?
> Here's the tender coming,
>> Off at Shields Bar.
> Here's the tender coming,
>> Full of men of war.
>
> Here's the tender coming,
>> Stealing of my dear;
>>> O, dear honey,
>> They'll ship you out of here,
> They'll ship you foreign,
>> For that is what it means.
> Here's the tender coming,
>> Full of red marines.

> From *A Sailor's Garland.*

A SEA DIRGE

> Full fathom five thy father lies:
>> Of his bones are coral made;
> Those are pearls that were his eyes:
>> Nothing of him that doth fade,

tender : a boat or other small vessel, that 'attends' a ship
with men, stores, etc.

But doth suffer a sea-change
Into something rich and strange.
Sea-nymphs hourly ring his knell:
Hark! now I hear them,
Ding, dong, bell.

SHAKESPEARE.

2. *Its Lawless Joys*

THE OLD BUCCANEER

Oh England is a pleasant place for them that's rich and high,
But England is a cruel place for such poor folks as I;
And such a port for mariners I ne'er shall see again
As the pleasant Isle of Avès, beside the Spanish main.

There were forty craft in Avès that were both swift and stout,
All furnished well with small arms and cannons round about;
And a thousand men in Avès made laws so fair and free
To choose their valiant captains and obey them loyally.

Thence we sailed against the Spaniard with
  his hoards of plate and gold,
Which he wrung with cruel tortures from
  Indian folk of old;
Likewise the merchant captains, with hearts
  as hard as stone,
Who flog men, and keel-haul them, and starve
  them to the bone.

O the palms grew high in Avès, and fruits that
  shone like gold,
And the colibris and parrots they were gorgeous
  to behold;
And the negro maids to Avès from bondage
  fast did flee,
To welcome gallant sailors, a-sweeping in from
  sea.

O sweet it was in Avès to hear the landward
  breeze,
A-swing with good tobacco in a net between
  the trees,
With a negro lass to fan you, while you listened
  to the roar
Of the breakers on the reef outside, that never
  touched the shore.

colibris. humming-birds.

But Scripture saith, an ending to all fine things
must be;
So the King's ships sailed on Avès, and quite
put down were we.
All day we fought like bulldogs, but they burst
the booms at night;
And I fled in a piragua, sore wounded, from the
fight.

Nine days I floated starving, and a negro lass
beside,
Till, for all I tried to cheer her, the poor young
thing she died;
But as I lay a-gasping, a Bristol sail came by,
And brought me home to England here, to
beg until I die.

And now I'm old and going—I'm sure I can't
tell where;
One comfort is, this world's so hard, I can't be
worse off there:
If I might but be a sea-dove, I'd fly across the
main,
To the pleasant Isle of Avès, to look at it
once again.

CHARLES KINGSLEY.

piragua : a " dug-out " canoe.

THE SALCOMBE SEAMAN'S FLAUNT TO THE
PROUD PIRATE

A lofty ship from Salcombe came,
  Blow high, blow low, and so sailed we ;
She had golden trucks that shone like flame,
  On the bonny coasts of Barbary.

"Masthead, masthead," the captains hail,
  Blow high, blow low, and so sailed we ;
"Look out and round, d'ye see a sail?"
  On the bonny coasts of Barbary.

"There's a ship that looms like Beachy Head,"
  Blow high, blow low, and so sailed we ;
"Her banner aloft it blows out red,"
  On the bonny coasts of Barbary.

"Oh, ship ahoy, and where do you steer?"
  Blow high, blow low, and so sailed we ;
"Are you man-of-war, or privateer?"
  On the bonny coasts of Barbary.

"I am neither one of the two," said she,
  Blow high, blow low, and so sailed we ;
"I'm a pirate, looking for my fee,"
  On the bonny coasts of Barbary.

trucks : mast-head caps.

"I'm a jolly pirate, out for gold:"
  Blow high, blow low, and so sailed we;
"I will rummage through your after hold,"
  On the bonny coasts of Barbary.

The grumbling guns they flashed and roared,
  Blow high, blow low, and so sailed we;
Till the pirate's masts went overboard,
  On the bonny coasts of Barbary.

They fired shots till the pirate's deck,
  Blow high, blow low, and so sailed we;
Was blood and spars and broken wreck,
  On the bonny coasts of Barbary.

"O do not haul the red flag down,"
  Blow high, blow low, and so sailed we;
"O keep all fast until we drown,"
  On the bonny coasts of Barbary.

They called for cans of wine, and drank,
  Blow high, blow low, and so sailed we;
They sang their songs until she sank,
  On the bonny coasts of Barbary.

Now let us brew good cans of flip,
  Blow high, blow low, and so sailed we;
And drink a bowl to the Salcombe ship,
  On the bonny coasts of Barbary.

And drink a bowl to the lad of fame,
  Blow high, blow low, and so sailed we ;
Who put the pirate ship to shame,
  On the bonny coasts of Barbary.

From A Sailor's Garland.

The Smuggler

O my true love's a smuggler and sails upon
    the sea,
And I would I were a seaman to go along with he;
To go along with he for the satins and the wine,
And run the tubs at Slapton when the stars
    do shine.

O Hollands is a good drink when the nights
    are cold,
And Brandy is a good drink for them as grows
    old.
There is lights in the cliff-top when the boats
    are home-bound,
And we run the tubs at Slapton when the word
    goes round.

The King he is a proud man in his grand red coat,
But I do love a smuggler in a little fishing-boat;
For he runs the Mallins lace and he spends his
    money free,
And I would I were a seaman to go along with he.

From A Sailor's Garland.

ARMS AND THE MAN

The generations pass, each in its turn wondering whether it is to be the one to see the ending of War and the awakening of the common sense of nations. But the Poetry of the glory of Battle, the hymning of high heroisms, the dirges for those who nobly died—these will remain, to gild its memory, long after the last echo of the last war-drum has faded out of the world.

THE MAID

Thunder of riotous hoofs over the quaking
   sod;
Clash of reeking squadrons, steel-capped, iron-
   shod;
The White Maid and the white horse, and the
   flapping banner of God.

Black hearts riding for money; red hearts
   riding for fame;
The Maid who rides for France and the King
   who rides for shame—
Gentlemen, fools, and a saint riding in Christ's
   high name!

"Dust to dust!" it is written. Wind-scattered are lance and bow.
Dust, the Cross of Saint George; dust, the banner of snow.
The bones of the King are crumbled, and rotted the shafts of the foe.

Forgotten, the young knight's valour; forgotten, the captain's skill;
Forgotten, the fear and the hate and the mailed hands raised to kill;
Forgotten, the shields that clashed and the arrows that cried so shrill.

Like a story from some old book, that battle of long ago:
Shadows, the poor French King and the might of his English foe;
Shadows, the charging nobles and the archers kneeling a-row—
But a flame in my heart and my eyes, the Maid with her banner of snow!

THEODORE ROBERTS.

The Eve of Waterloo

There was a sound of revelry by night,
  And Belgium's capital had gather'd then
Her Beauty and her Chivalry, and bright
  The lamps shone o'er fair women and brave
    men.
A thousand hearts beat happily; and when
  Music arose with its voluptuous swell,
Soft eyes look'd love to eyes which spake
  again,
And all went merry as a marriage-bell;
But hush! hark! a deep sound strikes like
  a rising knell!

Did ye not hear it?—No; 'twas but the wind,
  Or the car rattling o'er the stony street;
On with the dance! let joy be unconfined;
  No sleep till morn, when. Youth and
    Pleasure meet
To chase the glowing hours with flying feet.
  But hark!—that heavy sound breaks in
    once more,
As if the clouds its echo would repeat;
  And nearer, clearer, deadlier than before!
Arm! Arm! it is—it is—the cannon's opening
  roar!

Within a window'd niche of that high hall
    Sate Brunswick's fated chieftain; he did hear
That sound, the first amidst the festival,
    And caught its tone with Death's prophetic
        ear;
And when they smiled because he deem'd it
        near,
    His heart more truly knew that peal too well
Which stretch'd his father on a bloody bier,
    And rous'd the vengeance blood alone could
        quell:
He rush'd into the field, and, foremost fighting,
    fell.

Ah! then and there was hurrying to and fro,
    And gathering tears, and tremblings of dis-
        tress,
And cheeks all pale, which but an hour ago
    Blush'd at the praise of their own loveliness;
And there were sudden partings, such as press
    The life from out young hearts, and choking
        sighs
Which ne'er might be repeated: who would
        guess
    If ever more should meet those mutual eyes,
Since upon night so sweet such awful morn
    could rise!

And there was mounting in hot haste: the
    steed,
    The mustering squadron, and the clattering
    car,
Went pouring forward with impetuous speed,
    And swiftly forming in the ranks of war;
And the deep thunder peal on peal afar;
    And near, the beat of the alarming drum
Rous'd up the soldier ere the morning star;
    While throng'd the citizens with terror
    dumb,
Or whispering with white lips—"The foe!
    they come! they come!"

And wild and high the "Camerons' gathering"
    rose,
    The war-note of Lochiel, which Albyn's hills
Have heard, and heard, too, have her Saxon
    foes:
    How in the noon of night that pibroch thrills
Savage and shrill! But with the breath
    which fills
    Their mountain-pipe, so fill the moun-
    taineers
With the fierce native daring which instils
    The stirring memory of a thousand years,
And Evan's, Donald's fame rings in each
    clansman's ears!

And Ardennes waves above them her green
  leaves,
  Dewy with Nature's tear-drops, as they
    pass,
Grieving, if aught inanimate e'er grieves,
  Over the unreturning brave,—alas!
Ere evening to be trodden like the grass
  Which now beneath them, but above
    shall grow
In its next verdure, when this fiery mass
Of living valour, rolling on the foe,
And burning with high hope, shall moulder cold
    and low.

Last noon beheld them full of lusty life,
  Last eve in Beauty's circle proudly gay,
The midnight brought the signal-sound of
    strife,
  The morn the marshalling in arms,—the day
Battle's magnificently stern array!
  The thunder-clouds close o'er it, which
    when rent
The earth is cover'd thick with other clay,
  Which her own clay shall cover, heap'd
    and pent,
Rider and horse,—friend, foe,—in one red
    burial blent!

LORD BYRON.

THE GLORY THAT WAS GREECE

I include this among the War Poems, because it is a call to a conquered nation to rise in arms against their oppressors—a call that was in due course answered.

The isles of Greece! the isles of Greece!
  Where burning Sappho loved and sung,
Where grew the arts of war and peace,
  Where Delos rose, and Phoebus sprung!
Eternal summer gilds them yet,
But all except their sun is set.

The Scian and the Teian muse,
  The hero's harp, the lover's lute,
Have found the fame your shores refuse:
  Their place of birth alone is mute
To sounds which echo further west
Than your sires' "Islands of the Blest."

The mountains look on Marathon,
  And Marathon looks on the sea;
And, musing there an hour alone,
  I dreamed that Greece might still be free;
For, standing on the Persian's grave,
I could not deem myself a slave.

Scian and *Teian:* i.e. Homer and Anacreon.

A king sate on the rocky brow
  Which looks o'er sea-born Salamis;
And ships by thousands lay below,
  And men in nations;—all were his!
He counted them at break of day,
And when the sun set, where were they?

And where are they? and where art thou,
  My country?   On thy voiceless shore
The heroic lay is tuneless now,
  The heroic bosom beats no more!
And must thy lyre, so long divine,
Degenerate into hands like mine?

'Tis something in the dearth of fame,
  Though linked among the fettered race,
To feel at least a patriot's shame,
  Even as I sing, suffuse my face;
For what is left the poet here?
For Greeks a blush—for Greece a tear!

Must *we* but weep o'er days more blest?
  Must *we* but blush?   Our fathers bled.
Earth! render back from out thy breast
  A remnant of our Spartan dead!
Of the three hundred grant but three,
To make a new Thermopylæ!

What, silent still? and silent all?
　　Ah! no: the voices of the dead
Sound like a distant torrent's fall,
　　And answer, "Let one living head,
But one arise,—we come, we come!"
'Tis but the living who are dumb.

In vain—in vain; strike other chords;
　　Fill high the cup with Samian wine!
Leave battles to the Turkish hordes,
　　And shed the blood of Scio's vine!
Hark! rising to the ignoble call,
How answers each bold Bacchanal!

You have the Pyrrhic dance as yet;
　　Where is the Pyrrhic phalanx gone?
Of two such lessons, why forget
　　The nobler and the manlier one?
You have the letters Cadmus gave;
Think ye he meant them for a slave?

Fill high the bowl with Samian wine!
　　We will not think of themes like these!
It made Anacreon's song divine:
　　He served—but served Polycrates:
A tyrant; but our masters then
Were still, at least, our countrymen.

The tyrant of the Chersonese
   Was freedom's best and bravest friend;
That tyrant was Miltiades!
   Oh that the present hour would lend
Another despot of the kind!
Such chains as his were sure to bind.

Fill high the bowl with Samian wine!
   On Suli's rock and Parga's shore
Exists the remnant of a line
   Such as the Doric mothers bore;
And there, perhaps, some seed is sown
The Heracleidan blood might own.

Trust not for freedom to the Franks—
   They have a king who buys and sells;
In native swords and native ranks
   The only hope of courage dwells:
But Turkish force and Latin fraud
Would break your shield, however broad.

Fill high the bowl with Samian wine!
   Our virgins dance beneath the shade—
I see their glorious black eyes shine;
   But, gazing on each glowing maid,
My own the burning tear-drop laves,
To think such breasts must suckle slaves.

Place me on Sunium's marbled steep,
   Where nothing save the waves and I
May hear our mutual murmurs sweep;
   There, swan-like, let me sing and die:
A land of slaves shall ne'er be mine—
Dash down yon cup of Samian wine!

LORD BYRON.

BATTLE HYMN OF THE AMERICAN REPUBLIC

Mine eyes have seen the glory of the coming
   of the Lord:
He is trampling out the vintage where the
   grapes of wrath are stored;
He hath loosed the fatal lightning of his
   terrible swift sword:
     His truth is marching on.

I have seen him in the watch-fires of a hundred
   circling camps;
They have builded him an altar in the evening
   dews and damps;
I can read his righteous sentence by the dim
   and flaring lamps:
     His day is marching on.

He has sounded forth the trumpet that shall
   never call retreat;
He is sifting out the hearts of men before his
   Judgment Seat;
O, be swift, my soul to answer Him, be
   jubilant my feet!
      Our God is marching on.

In the beauty of the lilies Christ was born,
   across the sea,
With a glory in his bosom that transfigures
   you and me:
As he died to make men holy, let us die to
   make men free,
      While God is marching on.
            JULIA WARD HOWE.

TO LUCASTA, ON GOING TO THE WARS

   Tell me not, Sweet, I am unkind,
     That from the nunnery
   Of thy chaste breast and quiet mind
  . To war and arms I fly.

   True, a new mistress now I chase,
     The first foe in the field;
   And with a stronger faith embrace
     A sword, a horse, a shield.

Yet this inconstancy is such
  As you too shall adore;
I could not love thee, Dear, so much,
  Loved I not Honour more.

Richard Lovelace.

The Black Prince

O for the voice of that wild horn,
On Fontarabian echoes borne,
  The dying hero's call,
That told imperial Charlemagne
How Paynim sons of swarthy Spain
  Had wrought his champion's fall.

Sad over earth and ocean sounding,
And England's distant cliffs astounding,
  Such are the notes should say
How Britain's hope, and France's fear,
Victor of Cressy and Poitier,
  In Bordeaux dying lay.

"Raise my faint head, my squires," he said,
"And let the casement be displayed,
  That I may see once more
The splendour of the setting sun
Gleam on thy mirrored wave, Garonne,
  And Blay's empurpled shore.

"Like me, he sinks to Glory's sleep,
His fall the dews of evening steep,
   As if in sorrow shed.
So soft shall fall the trickling tear,
When England's maids and matrons hear
   Of their Black Edward dead.

"And though my sun of glory set,
Nor France nor England shall forget
   The terror of my name;
And oft shall Britain's heroes rise,
New planets in these southern skies,
   Through clouds of blood and flame."

SIR WALTER SCOTT.

THE BURIAL OF SIR JOHN MOORE

Not a drum was heard, not a funeral note,
   As his corse to the rampart we hurried;
Not a soldier discharged his farewell shot
   O'er the grave where our hero we buried.

We buried him darkly at dead of night,
   The sods with our bayonets turning,
By the struggling moonbeam's misty light
   And the lantern dimly burning.

No useless coffin enclosed his breast,
   Not in sheet or in shroud we wound him;
But he lay like a warrior taking his rest
   With his martial cloak around him.

Few and short were the prayers we said,
   And we spoke not a word of sorrow;
But we steadfastly gazed on the face of the
     dead,
   And we bitterly thought of the morrow.

We thought, as we hollow'd his narrow bed
   And smooth'd down his lonely pillow,
That the foe and the stranger would tread o'er
     his head,
   And we far away on the billow!

Lightly they'll talk of the spirit that's gone,
   And o'er his cold ashes upbraid him—
But little he'll reck, if they let him sleep on
   In the grave where a Briton has laid him.

But half of our heavy task was done
   When the clock struck the hour for retiring;
And we heard the distant and random gun
   That the foe was sullenly firing.

Slowly and sadly we laid him down,
  From the field of his fame fresh and gory;
We carved not a line, and we raised not a
    stone,
  But we left him alone with his glory.

CHARLES WOLFE.

How Sleep the Brave

How sleep the brave, who sink to rest
By all their country's wishes blest!
When Spring, with dewy fingers cold,
Returns to deck their hallowed mould,
She there shall dress a sweeter sod
Than Fancy's feet have ever trod.

By fairy hands their knell is rung;
By forms unseen their dirge is sung;
There Honour comes, a pilgrim grey,
To bless the turf that wraps their clay;
And Freedom shall awhile repair
To dwell, a weeping hermit, there!

WILLIAM COLLINS.

SOLDIER, REST!

Soldier, rest! thy warfare o'er,
  Sleep the sleep that knows not breaking!
Dream of battled fields no more,
  Days of danger, nights of waking.
In our isle's enchanted hall,
  Hands unseen thy couch are strewing,
Fairy strains of music fall,
  Every sense in slumber dewing.
Soldier, rest! thy warfare o'er,
Dream of fighting fields no more;
Sleep the sleep that knows not breaking,
Morn of toil, nor night of waking.

No rude sound shall reach thine ear,
  Armour's clang, or war-steed champing
Trump nor pibroch summon here
  Mustering clan, or squadron tramping.
Yet the lark's shrill fife may come
  At the daybreak from the fallow,
And the bittern sound his drum,
  Booming from the sedgy shallow.
Ruder sounds shall none be near,
Guards nor warders challenge here,
Here's no war-steed's neigh and champing,
Shouting clans, or squadrons stamping.

Huntsman, rest! thy chase is done;
   While our slumbrous spells assail ye,
Dream not, with the rising sun,
   Bugles here shall sound reveillé.
Sleep! the deer is in his den;
   Sleep! thy hounds are by thee lying;
Sleep! nor dream in yonder glen,
   How thy gallant steed lay dying.
Huntsman, rest! thy chase is done,
Think not of the rising sun,
For at dawning to assail ye,
Here no bugles sound reveillé.

SIR WALTER SCOTT.

THE OTHER SIDE OF IT

1. THE PATRIOT

It was roses, roses, all the way,
   With myrtle mixed in my path like mad:
The house-roofs seemed to heave and sway,
   The church-spires flamed, such flags they
         had,
A year ago on this very day.

The air broke into a mist with bells,
  The old walls rocked with the crowd and
    cries.
Had I said, "Good folk, mere noise repels—
  But give me your sun from yonder
    skies!"
They had answered, "And afterward, what
    else?"

Alack, it was I who leaped at the sun
  To give it my loving friends to keep!
Nought man could do, have I left undone:
  And you see my harvest, what I reap
This very day, now a year is run.

There's nobody on the house-tops now—
  Just a palsied few at the windows set;
For the best of the sight is, all allow,
  At the Shambles' Gate—or, better yet,
By the very scaffold's foot, I trow.

I go in the rain, and, more than needs,
  A rope cuts both my wrists behind;
And I think, by the feel, my forehead bleeds,
  For they fling, whoever has a mind,
Stones at me for my year's misdeeds.

Thus I entered, and thus I go!
   In triumphs, people have dropped down dead,
"Paid by the world, what dost thou owe
   Me?"—God might question; now instead,
'Tis God shall repay: I am safer so.

ROBERT BROWNING.

2.   FOR THOSE WHO FAIL

"All honour to him who shall win the prize,"
The world has cried for a thousand years;
But to him who tries and who fails and dies,
I give great honour and glory and tears.

O great is the hero who wins a name,
But greater many and many a time
Some pale-faced fellow who dies in shame,
And lets God finish the thought sublime.

And great is the man with a sword undrawn,
And good is the man who refrains from wine;
But the man who fails and yet fights on,
Lo he is the twin-born brother of mine!

JOAQUIN MILLER.

3. KEEPING ON

Say not the struggle nought availeth,
  The labour and the wounds are vain,
The enemy faints not, nor faileth,
  And as things have been they remain.

If hopes were dupes, fears may be liars;
  It may be, in yon smoke concealed,
Your comrades chase e'en now the fliers,
  And, but for you, possess the field.

For while the tired waves, vainly breaking,
  Seem here no painful inch to gain,
Far back, through creeks and inlets making,
  Comes silent, flooding in, the main.

And not by eastern windows only,
  When daylight comes, comes in the light;
In front the sun climbs slow, how slowly!
  But westward, look, the land is bright!

A. H. CLOUGH.

STORY-POEMS

THE LADY OF SHALOTT

I.

On either side the river lie
Long fields of barley and of rye,
That clothe the wold and meet the sky;
And through the field the road runs by
    To many-towered Camelot;
And up and down the people go,
Gazing where the lilies blow
Round an island there below,
    The island of Shalott.

Willows whiten, aspens quiver,
Little breezes dusk and shiver
Through the wave that runs for ever
By the island in the river
    Flowing down to Camelot.
Four gray walls, and four gray towers,
Overlook a space of flowers,
And the silent isle embowers
    The Lady of Shalott.

By the margin, willow-veil'd,
Slide the heavy barges trail'd
By slow horses; and unhail'd
The shallop flitteth silken-sail'd
   Skimming down to Camelot:
But who has seen her wave her hand?
Or at the casement seen her stand?
Or is she known in all the land,
   The Lady of Shalott?

Only reapers, reaping early
In among the bearded barley,
Hear a song that echoes cheerly
From the river winding clearly,
   Down to towered Camelot:
And by moon the reaper weary,
Piling sheaves in upland airy,
Listening, whispers, "'Tis the fairy
   Lady of Shalott."

II.

There she weaves by night and day
A magic web with colours gay.
She has heard a whisper say,
A curse is on her if she stay
   To look down to Camelot.

She knows not what the curse may be,
And so she weaveth steadily,
And little other care hath she,
    The Lady of Shalott.

And moving thro' a mirror clear
That hangs before her all the year,
Shadows of the world appear.
There she sees the highway near
    Winding down to Camelot:
There the river eddy whirls,
And there the surly village-churls,
And the red cloaks of market girls,
    Pass onward from Shalott.

Sometimes a troop of damsels glad,
An abbot on an ambling pad,
Sometimes a curly shepherd-lad,
Or long-hair'd page in crimson clad,
    Goes by to tower'd Camelot:
And sometimes through the mirror blue
The knights come riding two and two:
She hath no loyal knight and true,
    The Lady of Shalott.

But in her web she still delights
To weave the mirror's magic sights,

For often through the silent nights
A funeral, with plumes and lights
　And music, went to Camelot:
Or, when the moon was overhead,
Came two young lovers lately wed;
"I am half sick of shadows," said
　The Lady of Shalott.

III.

A bow-shot from her bower-eaves,
He rode between the barley-sheaves,
The sun came dazzling thro' the leaves,
And flamed upon the brazen greaves
　Of bold Sir Lancelot.
A red-cross knight for ever kneel'd
To a lady in his shield,
That sparkled on the yellow field
　Beside remote Shalott.

The gemmy bridle glitter'd free,
Like to some branch of stars we see
Hung in the golden Galaxy.
The bridle bells rang merrily
　As he rode down to Camelot:

　　　　greaves : leg-armour below the knee.
　　　　galaxy : the "Milky Way."

And from his blazon'd baldric slung
A mighty silver bugle hung,
And as he rode his armour rung,
  Beside remote Shalott.

All in the blue unclouded weather
Thick-jewell'd shone the saddle-leather,
The helmet and the helmet-feather
Burn'd like one burning flame together,
  As he rode down to Camelot.
As often thro' the purple night,
Below the starry clusters bright,
Some bearded meteor, trailing light,
  Moves over still Shalott.

His broad clear brow in sunlight glow'd;
On burnish'd hooves his war-horse trode;
From underneath his helmet flow'd
His coal-black curls as on he rode,
  As he rode down to Camelot.
From the bank and from the river
He flash'd into the crystal mirror,
"Tirra lirra," by the river
  Sang Sir Lancelot.

blazon'd baldric : a broad shoulder-belt painted heraldically.

She left the web, she left the loom,
She made three paces thro' the room,
She saw the water-lily bloom,
, She saw the helmet and the plume,
    She look'd down to Camelot.
. Out flew the web and floated wide;
The mirror crack'd from side to side;
"The curse is come upon me," cried
    The Lady of Shalott.

IV.

In the stormy east-wind straining,
The pale yellow woods were waning,
The broad stream in his banks complaining,
Heavily the low sky raining
    Over tower'd Camelot;
Down she came and found a boat
Beneath a willow left afloat,
And round about the prow she wrote
    The Lady of Shalott.

And down the river's dim expanse—
Like some bold seer in a trance,
Seeing all his own mischance—
. With a glassy countenance
    Did she look to Camelot.

And at the closing of the day
She loosed the chain and down she lay;
The broad stream bore her far away,
    The Lady of Shalott.

Lying, robed in snowy white
That loosely flew to left and right—
The leaves upon her falling light—
Thro' the noises of the night
    She floated down to Camelot:
And as the boat-head wound along
The willowy hills and fields among,
They heard her singing her last song,
    The Lady of Shalott.

Heard a carol, mournful, holy,
Chanted loudly, chanted lowly,
Till her blood was frozen slowly,
And her eyes were darken'd wholly,
    Turn'd to tower'd Camelot.
For ere she reached upon the tide
The first house by the water-side,
Singing in her song she died,
    The Lady of Shalott.

Under tower and balcony,
By garden-wall and gallery,

A gleaming shape she floated by,
Dead-pale between the houses high,
  Silent into Camelot.
Out upon the wharfs they came,
Knight and burgher, lord and dame,
And round the prow they read her name,
  The Lady of Shalott.

Who is this? and what is here?
And in the lighted palace near
Died the sound of royal cheer;
And they cross'd themselves for fear
  All the knights at Camelot:
But Lancelot mused a little space;
He said, "She has a lovely face;
God in his mercy lend her grace,
  The Lady of Shalott."
            ALFRED, LORD TENNYSON.

THE FORSAKEN MERMAN

Come, dear children, let us away;
  Down and away below.
Now my brothers call from the bay;
Now the great winds shoreward blow;
Now the salt tides seaward flow;

burgher : citizen.

Now the wild white horses play,
Champ and chafe and toss in the spray.
Children dear, let us away.
This way, this way!

Call her once before you go—
Call once yet!
In a voice that she will know:
"Margaret! Margaret!"
Children's voices should be dear
(Call once more) to a mother's ear;
Children's voices, wild with pain—
Surely she will come again!
Call her once and come away.
This way, this way!
"Mother dear, we cannot stay!"
The wild white horses foam and fret.
Margaret! Margaret!

Come, dear children, come away down.
Call no more.
One last look at the white-wall'd town,
And the little grey church on the windy shore.
Then come down.
She will not come though you call all day.
Come away, come away!

Children dear, was it yesterday
We heard the sweet bells over the bay?
In the caverns where we lay,
Through the surf and through the swell,
The far-off sound of a silver bell?
'Sand-strewn caverns, cool and deep,
Where the winds are all asleep;
Where the spent lights quiver and gleam;
Where the salt weed sways in the stream;
Where the sea-beasts, ranged all round,
Feed in the ooze of their pasture-ground;
Where the sea-snakes coil and twine,
Dry their mail and bask in the brine;
Where great whales come sailing by,
Sail and sail, with unshut eye,
Round the world for ever and aye?
When did music come this way?
Children dear, was it yesterday?

Children dear, was it yesterday
(Call yet once) that she went away?
Once she sate with you and me,
On a red gold throne in the heart of the sea,
And the youngest sate on her knee.
She combed its bright hair, and she tended it well,
When down swung the sound of a far-off bell.

5—2

She sigh'd, she look'd up through the clear
    green sea;
She said: "I must go, for my kinsfolk pray
In the little grey church on the shore to-day.
'Twill be Easter-time in the world—ah me!
And I lose my poor soul, Merman, here with
    thee."
I said, "Go up, dear heart, through the waves;
Say thy prayer, and come back to the kind
    sea-caves."
She smiled, she went up through the surf in
    the bay.
  Children dear, was it yesterday?

  Children dear, were we long alone?
"The sea grows stormy, the little ones moan.
Long prayers," I said, "in the world they
    say.
Come!" I said, and we rose through the surf
    in the bay.
We went up the beach, by the sandy down
Where the sea-stocks bloom, to the white-
    walled town.
Through the narrow paved streets, where all
    was still,
To the little grey church on the windy hill.

From the church came a murmur of folk at
    their prayers,
But we stood without in the cold blowing airs.
We climb'd on the graves, on the stones worn
    with rains,
And we gazed up the aisle through the small
    leaded panes.
    She sate by the pillar; we saw her clear:
    "Margaret, hist! come quick, we are here!
    Dear heart," I said, "we are long alone.
    The sea grows stormy, the little ones moan."
But, ah! she gave me never a look,
For her eyes were sealed to the holy book.
Loud prays the priest; shut stands the door.
    Come away, children, call no more.
    Come away, come down, call no more.

Down, down, down,
    Down to the depths of the sea!
She sits at her wheel in the humming town,
    Singing most joyfully.
Hark what she sings: "O joy, O joy,
For the humming street, and the child with its
    toy!
For the priest, and the bell, and the holy well;
    For the wheel where I spun,
    And the blessèd light of the sun!"

And so she sings her fill.
Singing most joyfully,
Till the spindle drops from her hand,
And the whizzing wheel stands still.
She steals to the window and looks at the sand,
And over the sand at the sea;
And her eyes are set in a stare;
And anon there breaks a sigh,
And anon there drops a tear,
From a sorrow-clouded eye,
And a heart sorrow-laden,
   A long, long sigh
For the cold strange eyes of a little Mermaiden
And the gleam of her golden hair.

Come away, away, children!
Come children, come down!
The hoarse wind blows coldly;
Lights shine in the town.
She will start from her slumber
When gusts shake the door;
She will hear the winds howling,
Will hear the waves roar.
We shall see, while above us
The waves roar and whirl,
A ceiling of amber,
A pavement of pearl.

Singing: "Here came a mortal,
But faithless was she:
And alone dwell for ever
The kings of the sea."

But, children, at midnight,
When soft the winds blow,
When clear falls the moonlight,
When spring-tides are low:
When sweet airs come seaward
From heaths starr'd with broom;
And high rocks throw mildly
On the blanch'd sands a gloom:
Up the still, glistening beaches,
Up the creeks we will hie,
Over banks of bright seaweed
The ebb-tide leaves dry.
We will gaze, from the sand-hills,
At the white, sleeping town;
At the church on the hill-side—
And then come back down.
Singing: "There dwells a loved one,
    But cruel is she.
She left lonely for ever
    The kings of the sea."

MATTHEW ARNOLD.

THE LEGEND BEAUTIFUL

"Hadst thou stayed, I must have fled!"
That is what the Vision said.

In his chamber all alone,
Kneeling on the floor of stone,
Prayed the Monk in deep contrition
For his sins of indecision,
Prayed for greater self-denial
In temptation and in trial;
It was noonday by the dial,
And the Monk was all alone.

Suddenly, as if it lighten'd,
An unwonted splendour brighten'd
All within him and without him
In that narrow cell of stone;
And he saw the Blessed Vision
Of our Lord, with light Elysian
Like a vesture wrapped about him,
Like a garment round him thrown.

Not as crucified and slain,
Not in agonies of pain,
Not with bleeding hands and feet,
Did the Monk his Master see;

Elysian : heavenly.

But as in the village street,
In the house or harvest-field,
Halt and lame and blind he healed,
When he walkéd in Galilee.

In an attitude imploring,
Hands upon his bosom crossed,
Wondering, worshipping, adoring,
Knelt the Monk in rapture lost.
Lord, he thought, in heaven that reignest,
Who am I, that thus thou deignest
To reveal thyself to me?
Who am I, that from the centre
Of thy glory thou shouldst enter
This poor cell, my guest to be?

Then amid his exaltation,
Loud the convent bell appalling,
From its belfry calling, calling,
Rang through court and corridor
With persistent iteration
He had never heard before.
It was now the appointed hour
When alike in sun or shower,
Winter's cold or summer's heat,
To the convent portals came
All the blind and halt and lame,
All the beggars of the street.

For their daily dole of food
Dealt them by the brotherhood;
And their almoner was he
Who upon his bended knee,
Rapt in silent ecstasy
Of divinest self-surrender,
Saw the Vision and the Splendour.

Deep distress and hesitation
Mingled with his adoration;
Should he go or should he stay?
Should he leave the poor to wait
Hungry at the convent gate,
Till the Vision passed away?
Should he slight his radiant guest,
Slight his visitant celestial,
For a crowd of raggéd, bestial
Beggars at the convent gate?
Would the Vision there remain?
Would the Vision come again?

Then a voice within his breast
Whispered, audible and clear,
As if to the outward ear:
"Do thy duty; that is best;
Leave unto thy Lord the rest!"

almoner : giver of alms or charity.

Straightway to his feet he started,
And with longing look intent
On the Blessed Vision bent,
Slowly from his cell departed,
Slowly on his errand went.

At the gate the poor were waiting,
Looking through the iron grating,
With that terror in the eye
That is only seen in those
Who amid their wants and woes
Hear the sound of doors that close,
And of feet that pass them by;
Grown familiar with disfavour,
Grown familiar with the savour
Of the bread by which men die!
But to-day, they knew not why,
Like the gate of Paradise
Seemed the convent gate to rise,
Like a sacrament divine
Seemed to them the bread and wine.
In his heart the Monk was praying,
Thinking of the homeless poor,
What they suffer and endure;
What we see not, what we see;
And the inward voice was saying:

"Whatsoever thing thou doest
To the least of mine and lowest,
That thou doest unto me!"

Unto me! but had the Vision
Come to him in beggar's clothing,
Come a mendicant imploring,
Would he then have knelt adoring,
Or have listened with derision,
And have turned away with loathing?

Thus his conscience put the question,
Full of troublesome suggestion,
As at length, with hurried pace,
Towards his cell he turned his face,
And beheld the convent bright
With a supernatural light,
Like a luminous cloud expanding
Over floor and wall and ceiling.

But he paused with awe-struck feeling
At the threshold of his door,
For the Vision still was standing
As he left it there before,
When the convent bell appalling,
From its belfry calling, calling,
Summoned him to feed the poor.

Through the long hour-intervening
It had waited his return,
And he felt his bosom burn,
Comprehending all the meaning,
When the Blessed Vision said,
"Hadst thou stayed, I must have fled!"

H. W. LONGFELLOW.

ABOU BEN ADHEM

Abou Ben Adhem (may his tribe increase!)
Awoke one night from a deep dream of peace,
And saw, within the moonlight in his room,
Making it rich, and like a lily in bloom,
An angel writing in a book of gold :—
Exceeding peace had made Ben Adhem bold,
And to the presence in the room he said,
"What writest thou?"—The vision rais'd its
    head,
And with a look made all of sweet accord,
Answer'd, "The names of those that love the
    Lord."
"And is mine one?" said Abou. "Nay, not so,"
Replied the angel. Abou spoke more low,
But cheerly still; and said, "I pray thee, then,
Write me as one that loves his fellow men."

The angel wrote, and vanished. The next
   night
It came again with a great wakening light,
And show'd the names whom love of God had
   blest,
And lo! Ben Adhem's name led all the rest.

Leigh Hunt.

The Sands of Dee

"O Mary, go and call the cattle home,
   And call the cattle home,
   And call the cattle home,
     Across the sands of Dee";
The western wind was wild and dank with
   foam,
   And all alone went she.

The western tide crept up along the sand,
   And o'er and o'er the sand,
   And round and round the sand,
     As far as eye could see.
The rolling mist came down and hid the
   land:
   And never home came she.

"O is it weed, or fish, or floating hair—
  A tress of golden hair,
  A drownèd maiden's hair,
  Above the nets at sea?"
Was never salmon yet that shone so fair
  Among the stakes of Dee.

They rowed her in across the rolling foam,
  The cruel crawling foam,
  The cruel hungry foam,
  To her grave beside the sea.
But still the boatmen hear her call the cattle
    home,
  Across the sands of Dee.

CHARLES KINGSLEY.

LOCHINVAR

O young Lochinvar is come out of the west,
Through all the wide Border his steed was the
    best,
And save his good broad-sword he weapons
    had none;
He rode all unarmed, and he rode all alone.
So faithful in love, and so dauntless in war,
There never was knight like the young Loch-
    invar.

He stay'd not for brake, and he stopp'd not for
    stone,
He swam the Esk river where ford there was
    none;
But, ere he alighted at Netherby gate,
The bride had consented, the gallant came late:
For a laggard in love, and a dastard in war,
Was to wed the fair Ellen of brave Lochinvar.

So boldly he entered the Netherby Hall,
Among bride's-men and kinsmen, and brothers
    and all:
Then spoke the bride's father, his hand on his
    sword
(For the poor craven bridegroom said never a
    word),
"O come ye in peace here, or come ye in war,
Or to dance at our bridal, young Lord Loch-
    invar?"

"I long wooed your daughter, my suit you
    denied:—
Love swells like the Solway, but ebbs like its
    tide—
And now I am come, with this lost love of
    mine
To lead but one measure, drink one cup of wine.

There are maidens in Scotland more lovely by
    far.
That would gladly be bride to the young Loch-
    invar."
The bride kiss'd the goblet; the knight took
    it up,
He quaff'd off the wine, and he threw down the
    cup;
She look'd down to blush, and she look'd up
    to sigh,
With a smile on her lips and a tear in her eye.
He took her soft hand, ere her mother could
    bar,—
"Now tread we a measure!" said young Loch-
    invar.
So stately his form, and so lovely her face,
That never a hall such a galliard did grace;
While her mother did fret, and her father did
    fume,
And the bridegroom stood dangling his bonnet
    and plume;
And the bride-maidens whisper'd, "'Twere
    better by far
To have match'd our fair cousin with young
    Lochinvar."

galliard : a gay dance.

One touch to her hand and one word in her
    ear,
When they reach'd the hall door and the
    charger stood near;
So light to the croupe the fair lady he swung,
So light to the saddle before her he sprung!
"She is won! we are gone, over bank, bush,
    and scaur;
They'll have fleet steeds that follow," quoth
    young Lochinvar.

There was mounting 'mong Graemes of the
    Netherby clan;
Forsters, Fenwicks, and Musgraves, they rode
    and they ran:
There was racing and chasing on Cannobie Lee,
But the lost bride of Netherby ne'er did they
    see.
So daring in love, and so dauntless in war,
Have ye e'er heard of gallant like young Loch-
    invar?

Sir Walter Scott.

scaur : a steep bank.

DAY-DREAMS

This section will appeal to girls rather than to boys.
And yet day-dreams are no bad things for either sex—
just now and again, as a getting away from realities.

DREAMS TO SELL

If there were dreams to sell,
　What would you buy?
Some cost a passing bell;
　Some a light sigh,
That shakes from Life's fresh crown
Only a rose-leaf down.
If there were dreams to sell,
Merry and sad to tell,
And the crier rang the bell,
　What would you buy?

A cottage lone and still,
　With bowers nigh,
Shadowy, my woes to still,
　Until I die.
Such pearl from Life's fresh crown
Fain would I shake me down.
Were dreams to have at will,
This would best heal my ill,
　This would I buy.

T. L. BEDDOES.

6—2

THE LOST BOWER

> In the pleasant orchard closes,
> "God bless all our gains," say we;
> But "May God bless all our losses,"
> Better suits with our degree.—
> Listen gentle—ay, and simple! Listen children
> on the knee!

> Green the land is where my daily
> Steps in jocund childhood played—
> Dimpled close with hill and valley,
> Dappled very close with shade;
> Summer-snow of apple blossoms, running up
> from glade to glade.

> There is one hill I see nearer,
> In my vision of the rest;
> And a little wood seems clearer,
> As it climbeth from the west,
> Sideway from the tree-locked valley, to the
> airy upland crest.

> Small the wood is, green with hazels,
> And, completing the ascent,
> Where the wind blows and sun dazzles,
> Thrills in leafy tremblement:
> Like a heart that, after climbing, beateth
> quickly through content.

Not a step the wood advances
O'er the open hill-top's bound:
There, in green arrest, the branches
See their image on the ground:
You may walk between) them smiling, glad
  with sight and glad with sound.

For you hearken on your right hand,
How the birds do leap and call
In the greenwood, out of sight and
Out of reach and fear of all;
And the squirrels crack the filberts, through
  their cheerful madrigal.

On your left, the sheep are cropping
The slant grass and daisies pale;
And five apple-trees stand, dropping
Separate shadows toward the vale,
Over which, in choral silence, the hills look you
  their "All hail!"

Yet in childhood little prized I
That fair walk and far survey;
'Twas a straight walk, unadvised by
The least mischief worth a nay—
Up and down—as dull as grammar on an eve
  of holiday!

But the wood, all close and clenching
Bough in bough and root in root,—
No more sky (for over-branching)
At your head than at your foot,—
Oh, the wood drew me within it, by a glamour
   past dispute!

Few and broken paths showed through it,
Where the sheep had tried to run,—
Forced with snowy wool to strew it
Round the thickets, when anon
They with silly thorn-pricked noses bleated
   back into the sun.

But my childish heart beat stronger
Than those thickets dared to grow:
I could pierce them! *I* could longer
Travel on, methought, than so!
Sheep for sheep-paths! braver children climb
   and creep where they would go.

On a day, such pastime keeping,
With a fawn's heart debonair,
Under-crawling, overleaping
Thorns that prick and boughs that bear,
I stood suddenly astonished—I was gladdened
   unaware!

From the place I stood in, floated
Back the covert dim and close;
And the open ground was suited
Carpet-smooth with grass and moss,
And the blue-bell's purple presence signed it
worthily across.

'Twas a bower for garden fitter,
Than for any woodland wide!
Though a fresh and dewy glitter
Struck it through, from side to side,
Shaped and shaven was the freshness, as by
garden-cunning plied.   ·

Rose-trees, either side the door, were
Growing lithe and growing tall;
Each one set a summer warder
For the keeping of the hall,—
With a red rose, and a white rose, leaning,
nodding at the wall.

As I entered—mosses hushing
Stole all noises from my foot:
And a round elastic cushion,
Clasped within the linden's root,
Took me in a chair of silence, very rare and
absolute.

So, young muser, I sat listening
To my Fancy's wildest word—
On a sudden, through the glistening
Leaves around, a little stirred,
Came a sound, a sense of music, which was
    rather felt than heard.

Softly, finely, it inwound me—
From the world it shut me in,—
Like a fountain falling round me,
Which with silver waters thin
Clips a little marble Naiad, sitting smilingly
    within.

Whence the music came, who knoweth?
I know nothing. But indeed
Pan or Faunus never bloweth
So much sweetness from a reed
Which has sucked the milk of waters, at the
    oldest river-head.

Never lark the sun can waken
With such sweetness! when the lark,
The high planets overtaking
In the half-evanished Dark,
Casts his singing to their singing, like an arrow
    to the mark.

Never nightingale so singeth—
Oh! she leans on thorny tree,
And her poet-soul she flingeth
Over pain to victory!
Yet she never sings such music,—or she sings
it not to me!

Never blackbirds, never thrushes,
Nor small finches sing as sweet,
When the sun strikes through the bushes
To their crimson clinging feet,
And their pretty eyes look sideways to the
summer heavens complete.

In a child-abstraction lifted,
Straightway from the bower I passed;
Foot and soul being dimly drifted
Through the greenwood, till, at last,
In the hill-top's open sunshine, I all consciously
was cast.

And I said within me, laughing,
I have found a bower to-day,
A green lusus—fashioned half in
Chance, and half in Nature's play—
And a little bird sings nigh it, I will never more
missay.

lusus · a sport, a freak.

Henceforth, *I* will be the fairy
Of this bower, not built by one;
I will go there, sad or merry,
With each morning's benison;
And the bird shall be my harper in the dream-
hall I have won.

So I said.   But the next morning,
(—Child, look up into my face—
'Ware, O sceptic, of your scorning!
This is truth in its pure grace;)
The next morning, all had vanished, or my
wandering missed the place.

Day by day, with new desire,
Toward my wood I ran in faith—
Under leaf and over brier—
Through the thickets, out of breath—
Like the prince who rescued Beauty from the
sleep as long as death.

But his sword of mettle clashèd,
And his arm smote strong, I ween;
And her dreaming spirit flashèd
Through her body's fair white screen,
And the light thereof might guide him up the
cedarn alleys green.

But for me, I saw no splendour—
All my sword was my child-heart;
And the wood refused surrender
Of that bower it held apart,
Safe as Œdipus's grave-place, 'mid Colone's
olives swart.

I have lost—oh many a pleasure—
Many a hope, and many a power—
Studious health and merry leisure—
The first dew on the first flower!
But the first of all my losses was the losing of
the bower.

All my losses did I tell you,
Ye, perchance, would look away;—
Ye would answer me, "Farewell! you
Make sad company to-day;
And your tears are falling faster than the
bitter words you say."

For God placed me like a dial
In the open ground, with power;
And my heart had for its trial,
All the sun and all the shower!
And I suffered many losses; and my first was
of the bower.

ELIZABETH BARRETT BROWNING.

Echo and the Ferry

Ay, Oliver! I was but seven, and he was eleven;
He looked at me pouting and rosy. I blushed
    where I stood.
They had told us to play in the orchard (and I
    only seven!
A small guest at the farm); but he said, "Oh,
    a girl was no good,"
So he whistled and went, he went over the
    stile to the wood.
It was sad, it was sorrowful! Only a girl—
    only seven!
At home in the dark London smoke I had not
    found it out.
The pear trees looked on in their white, and
    blue birds flashed about;
And they too were angry as Oliver. Were
    they eleven?
I thought so. Yes, every one else was eleven
    —eleven!

So Oliver went, but the cowslips were tall at
    my feet,
And all the white orchard with fast-falling
    blossom was littered,
And under and over the branches those little
    birds twittered,

While hanging head downwards they scolded
   (because I was seven.
A pity. A very great pity. One should be eleven.
But soon I was happy, the smell of the world
   was so sweet.
And I saw a round hole in an apple-tree rosy
   and old.
Then I knew! for I peeped, and I felt it was
   right they should scold!
Eggs small and eggs many. For gladness I
   broke into laughter;
And then some one else—oh, how softly! came
   after, came after
With laughter—with laughter came after.

So this was the country; clear dazzle of azure
   and shiver
And whisper of leaves, and a humming all over
   the tall
White branches, a humming of bees. And I
   came to the wall—
A little low wall—and looked over, and there
   was the river,
The lane that led on to the village, and then
   the sweet river.
Clear-shining and slow, she had far far to go
   from her snow;

But each rush gleamed a sword in the sunlight
    to guard her long flow,
And she murmured, methought, with a speech
    very soft, very low—
"The ways will be long, but the days will be
    long," quoth the river,
"To me a long liver, long, long!" quoth the
    river—the river.

I dreamed of the country that night, of the
    orchard, the sky,
The voice that had mocked coming after and
    over and under.
But at last—in a day or two namely—Eleven
    and I
Were very fast friends, and to him I confided
    the wonder.
He said that was Echo. "Was Echo a wise
    kind of bee
That had learned how to laugh: could it laugh
    in one's ear and then fly,
And laugh again yonder?" "No; Echo"—he
    whispered it low—
"Was a woman, they said, but a woman whom
    no one could see
And no one could find; and he did not believe
    it, not he,

But he could not get near for the river that
    held us asunder.
Yet I that had money—a shilling, a whole
    silver shilling—
We might cross if I thought I would spend it."
    "Oh yes, I was willing"—
And we ran hand in hand, we ran down to the
    ferry, the ferry,
And we heard how she mocked at the folk
    with a voice clear and merry
When they called for the ferry; but oh! she
    was very—was very
Swift-footed. She spoke and was gone; and
    when Oliver cried,
"Hie over! hie over! you man of the ferry—
    the ferry!"
By the still water's side she was heard far and
    wide—she replied,
And she mocked in her voice sweet and merry
    "You man of the ferry,
You man of—you man of the ferry!"

"Hie over!" he shouted. The ferryman came
    at his calling,
Across the clear reed-bordered river he ferried
    us fast;—

Such a chase! Hand in hand, foot to foot,
    we ran on; it surpassed
All measure her doubling—so close, then so
    far away falling,
Then gone, and no more. Oh! to see her but
    once unaware,
And the mouth that had mocked, but we might
    not (yet sure she was there!)
Nor behold her wild eyes and her mystical
    countenance fair.

We sought in the wood, and we found the wood-
    wren in her stead;
In the field, and we found but the cuckoo that
    talked overhead;
By the brook, and we found the reed-sparrow
    deep-nested, in brown—
Not Echo, fair Echo! for Echo, sweet Echo!
    was flown.

So we came to the place where the dead people
    wait till God call.
The church was among them, grey moss over
    roof, over wall.
Very silent, so low. And we stood on a green
    grassy mound

And looked in at a window, for Echo, perhaps, in her round
Might have come in to hide there. But no; every oak carven seat
Was empty. We saw the great Bible—old, old, very old,
And the parson's great Prayer-book beside it; we heard the slow beat
Of the pendulum swing in the tower; we saw the clear gold
Of a sunbeam float down to the aisle and then waver and play
On the low chancel step and the railing, and Oliver said,
"Look, Katie! Look, Katie! when Lettice came here to be wed
She stood where that sunbeam drops down, and all white was her gown;
And she stepped upon flowers they strewed for her." Then quoth small Seven,
"Shall I wear a white gown and have flowers to walk upon ever?"

All doubtful: "It takes a long time to grow up," quoth Eleven;
"You're so little, you know, and the church is so old, it can never

Last on till you're tall." And in whispers—
    because it was old,
And holy, and fraught with strange meaning,
    half felt, but not told,
Full of old parsons' prayers, who were dead,
    of old days, of old folk
Neither heard nor beheld, but about us, in
    whispers we spoke.
Then we went from it softly, and ran hand in
    hand to the strand,
While bleating of flocks and birds piping made
    sweeter the land,
And Echo came back e'en as Oliver drew to
    the ferry,
"O Katie!" "O Katie!" "Come on, then!"
    "Come on, then!" "For, see,
The round sun, all red, lying low by the tree"
    —"by the tree."
"By the tree." Ay, she mocked him again,
    with her voice sweet and merry:
"Hie over!" "Hie over!" "You man of
    the ferry"—"the ferry."
"You man of the ferry—you man of—you man
    of—the ferry."

Ay, here—it was here that we woke her, the
    Echo of old;

All life of that day seems an echo, and many
    times told.
Shall I cross by the ferry to-morrow, and come
    in my white .
To that little old church? and will Oliver meet
    me anon?
Will it all seem an echo from childhood passed
    over—passed on?
Will the grave parson bless us? Hark, hark!
    in the dim failing light
I hear her! As then the child's voice clear
    and high, sweet and merry
Now she mocks the man's tone with "Hie
    over! Hie over the ferry!"
"And Katie." "And Katie." "Art out with
    the glowworms to-night,
My Katie?" "My Katie." For gladness I
    break into laughter
And tears. Then it all comes again as from
    far-away years;
Again, some one else—Oh, how softly!—with
    laughter comes after,
Comes after—with laughter comes after.

JEAN INGELOW.

POOR SUSAN'S DREAM

At the corner of Wood Street, when daylight
    appears,
Hangs a thrush that sings loud, it has sung for
    three years:
Poor Susan has passed by the spot, and has
    heard
In the silence of morning the song of the
    bird.

'Tis a note of enchantment; what ails her?
    She sees
A mountain ascending, a vision of trees;
Bright volumes of vapour through Lothbury
    glide,
And a river flows on through the vale of Cheap-
    side.

Green pastures she views in the midst of the
    dale
Down which she so often has tripp'd with her
    pail;
And a single small cottage, a nest like a
    dove's,
The one only dwelling on earth that she
    loves.

She looks, and her heart is in heaven: but
   they fade,
The mist and the river, the hill and the shade;
The stream will not flow, and the hill will not
   rise,
And the colours have all passed away from
   her eyes!

WILLIAM WORDSWORTH.

FANCY

   Tell me where is Fancy bred,
   Or in the heart or in the head?
   How begot, how nourishèd?
      Reply, reply.
   It is engender'd in the eyes,
   With gazing fed; and Fancy dies
   In the cradle where it lies.
     Let us all ring Fancy's knell:
     I'll begin it,—Ding, dong, bell.
   Ding, dong, bell.

SHAKESPEARE.

TWO HOME-COMINGS

1. The Good Woman Made Welcome in Heaven

Angels, thy old friends, there shall greet thee,
Glad at their own home now to meet thee.
All thy good works which went before,
And waited for thee at the door,
Shall own thee there; and all in one
Weave a constellation
Of crowns, with which the King, thy spouse,
Shall build up thy triumphant brows.
All thy old woes shall now smile on thee,
And thy pains sit bright upon thee:
All thy sorrows here shall shine,
And thy sufferings be divine.
Tears shall take comfort, and turn gems,
And wrongs repent to diadems.
Even thy deaths shall live, and new
Dress the soul which late they slew.
Thy wounds shall blush to such bright scars
As keep account of the Lamb's wars.

RICHARD CRASHAW.

2. THE SOLDIER RELIEVED

I'd like now, yet had haply been afraid,
To have just looked, when this man came to
    die,
And seen who lined the clean gay .garret
    sides,
And stood about the neat low truckle-bed,
With the heavenly manner of relieving guard.
Here had been, mark, the general-in-chief,
Thro' a whole campaign of the world's life and
    death,
Doing the King's work all the dim day long,
In his old coat and up to knees in mud,
Smoked like a herring, dining on a crust,—
And, now the day was won, relieved at once!
No further show or need of that old coat,
You are sure, for one thing! Bless us, all the
    while
How sprucely we are dressed out, you and I!
A second, and the angels alter that.

ROBERT BROWNING.

WHEN KNIGHTS WERE BOLD

HUNTING SONG

Waken, lords and ladies gay,
On the mountain dawns the day,
All the jolly chase is here,
With horse, and hawk, and hunting spear!
Hounds are in their couples yelling,
Hawks are whistling, horns are knelling.
Merrily, merrily, mingle they,
"Waken, lords and ladies gay."

Waken, lords and ladies gay,
The mist has left the mountain grey,
Springlets in the dawn are steaming,
Diamonds on the brake are gleaming,
And foresters have busy been
To track the buck in thicket green;
Now we come to chant our lay,
"Waken, lords and ladies gay."

Waken, lords and ladies gay,
To the greenwood haste away;
We can show you where he lies,
Fleet of foot, and tall of size;

knelling: sounding like a bell.   *brake:* fern, bracken

We can show the marks he made
When 'gainst the oak his antlers frayed;
You shall see him brought to bay;
"Waken, lords and ladies gay."

Louder, louder chant the lay,
Waken, lords and ladies gay!
Tell them youth, and mirth, and glee,
Run a course as well as we;
Time, stern huntsman! who can baulk,
Stanch as hound, and fleet as hawk?
Think of this, and rise with day,
Gentle lords and ladies gay!

Sir Walter Scott.

The Riding to the Tournament

Over meadows purple-flowered,
Through the dark lanes oak-embowered,
Over commons dry and brown,
Through the silent red-roofed town,
Past the reapers and the sheaves,
Over white roads strewn with leaves,
By the gipsy's ragged tent,
Rode we to the Tournament.

antlers : horns.

Over clover wet with dew,
Whence the sky-lark, startled, flew,
Through brown fallows, where the hare
Leapt up from its subtle lair,
Past the mill-stream and the reeds
Where the stately heron feeds,
By the warren's sunny wall,
Where the dry leaves shake and fall,
By the hall's ancestral trees,
Bent and writhing in the breeze,
Rode we all with one intent,
Gaily to the Tournament.

Golden sparkles, flashing gem,
Lit the robes of each of them,
Cloak of velvet, robe of silk,
Mantle snowy-white as milk,
Rings upon our bridle-hand,
Jewels on our belt and band,
Bells upon our golden reins,
Tinkling spurs and shining chains—
In such merry mob we went
Riding to the Tournament.

Laughing voices, scraps of song,
Lusty music loud and strong,
Rustling of the banners blowing,
Whispers as of rivers flowing.

Whistle of the hawks we bore
As they rise and as they soar,
Now and then a clash of drums
As the rabble louder hums,
Now and then a burst of horns
Sounding over brooks and bourns,
As in merry guise we went
Riding to the Tournament.

There were abbots fat and sleek,
Nuns in couples, pale and meek,
Jugglers tossing cups and knives,
Yeomen with their buxom wives,
Pages playing with the curls
Of the rosy village girls,
Grizzly knights with faces scarred,
Staring through their vizors barred,
Huntsmen cheering with a shout
At the wild stag breaking out,
Harper, stately as a king,
Touching now and then a string,
As our revel laughing went
To the solemn Tournament.

Charger with the massy chest,
Foam-spots flecking mane and breast,
Pacing stately, pawing ground,
Fretting for the trumpet's sound,

White and sorrel, roan and bay,
Dappled, spotted, black, and grey,
Palfreys snowy as the dawn,
Ponies sallow as the fawn,
All together neighing went
Trampling to the Tournament.

Long hair scattered in the wind,
Curls that flew a yard behind,
Flags that struggled like a bird
Chained and restive—not a word
But half buried in a laugh;
And the lance's gilded staff
Shaking when the bearer shook
At the jester's merry look,
As he grins upon his mule,
Like an urchin leaving school,
Shaking bauble, tossing bells,
At the merry jest he tells,—
So in happy mood we went,
Laughing to the Tournament.

What a bustle at the inn,
What a stir, without—within;
Filling flagons, brimming bowls
For a hundred thirsty souls;
Froth in snow-flakes flowing down,
From the pitcher big and brown,

While the tankards brim and bubble
With the balm for human trouble;
How the maiden coyly sips,
How the yeoman wipes his lips,
How the old knight drains the cup
Slowly and with calmness up,
And the abbot, with a prayer,
Fills the silver goblet rare,
Praying to the saints for strength
As he holds it at arm's length;
How the jester spins the bowl
On his thumb, then quaffs the whole;
How the pompous steward bends
And bows to half-a-dozen friends,
As in a thirsty mood we went
Duly to the Tournament.

Then again the country over
Through the stubble and the clover,
By the crystal-dropping springs,
Where the road dust clogs and clings
To the pearl-leaf of the rose,
Where the tawdry nightshade blows,
And the bramble twines its chains
Through the sunny village lanes,
Where the thistle sheds its seed,
And the goldfinch loves to feed,

By the milestone green with moss,
By the broken wayside cross,
In a merry band we went
Shouting to the Tournament.

Pilgrims with their hood and cowl,
Pursy burghers cheek by jowl,
Archers with their peacock's wing
Fitting to the waxen string,
Pedlars with their pack and bags,
Beggars with their coloured rags,
Silent monks, whose stony eyes
Rest in trance upon the skies,
Children sleeping at the breast,
Merchants from the distant West,
All in gay confusion went
To the royal Tournament.

Players with the painted face
And a drunken man's grimace,
Grooms who praise their raw-boned steeds,
Old wives telling maple beads,—
Blackbirds from the hedges broke,
Black crows from the beeches croak,
Glossy swallows in dismay
From the mill-stream fled away,
The angry swan, with ruffled breast,

Frowned upon her osier nest,
The wren hopped restless on the brake,
The otter made the sedges shake,
The butterfly before our rout
Flew like a blossom blown about;
The coloured leaves, a globe of life,
Spun round and scattered as in strife,
Sweeping down the narrow lane
Like the slant shower of the rain,
The lark in terror, from the sod,
Flew up and straight appealed to God,
As a noisy band we went
Trotting to the Tournament.

But when we saw the holy town,
With its river and its down,
Then the drums began to beat
And the flutes piped mellow sweet;
Then the deep and full bassoon
Murmured like a wood in June,
And the fifes, so sharp and bleak,
All at once began to speak.
Hear the trumpets clear and loud,
Full-tongued, eloquent and proud,
And the dulcimer that ranges
Through such wild and plaintive changes;

Merry sounds the jester's shawm,
To our gladness giving form;
And the shepherd's chalumeau,
Rich and soft and sad and low;
Hark! the bagpipes squeak and groan—
Every herdsman has his own;
So in measured step we went
Pacing to the Tournament.

All at once the chimes break out,
Then we hear the townsmen shout,
And the morris-dancers' bells
Tinkling in the grassy dells;
The bell thunder from the tower
Adds its sound of doom and power,
As the cannon's loud salute
For a moment made us mute;
Then again the laugh and joke
On the startled silence broke;—
Thus in merry mood we went
Laughing to the Tournament.

G. W. THORNBURY.

shawm . reed pipe.   *chalumeau :* reed pipe.

VARIOUS

A Red, Red Rose

O, my love is like a red, red rose,
    That's newly sprung in June:
O, my love is like the melody
    That's sweetly play'd in tune.

As fair art thou, my bonnie lass,
    So deep in love am I,
And I will love thee still, my dear,
    Till all the seas gang dry.

Till all the seas gang dry, my dear,
    And the rocks melt wi' the sun!
And I will love thee still, my dear,
    While the sands o' life shall run.

And fare thee well, my only love,
    And fare thee well a while!
And I will come again, my love,
    Tho' it were ten thousand mile!

                    Robert Burns.

gang : go.

BLOW, BUGLE, BLOW

The splendour falls on castle walls
And snowy summits old in story:
The long light shakes across the lakes,
And the wild cataract leaps in glory.
Blow, bugle, blow, set the wild echoes flying,
Blow, bugle; answer, echoes, dying, dying,
dying.

O hark, O hear! how thin and clear,
And thinner, clearer, farther going!
O sweet and far from cliff and scar
The horns of Elfland faintly blowing!
Blow, let us hear the purple glens replying:
Blow, bugle; answer, echoes, dying, dying,
dying.

O love, they die in yon rich sky,
They faint on hill or field or river:
Our echoes roll from soul to soul,
And grow for ever and for ever.
Blow, bugle, blow, set the wild echoes flying,
And answer, echoes, answer, dying, dying,
dying.

ALFRED, LORD TENNYSON.

scar : a crag, a precipice.

WEST AND EAST

Rome is chiefly known to young readers through the medium of Macaulay's spirited " Lays," which, however, are only a re-telling, in English ballad form, of some of the legends which survived into historical times concerning the infant city, about which nothing certain is known. They give no idea of the Rome of history, the world-power, or of the brooding immensity of her influence through centuries. This and the following poem illustrate, to some slight extent, the later Rome.

In his cool hall, with haggard eyes,
  The Roman-noble lay;
He drove abroad, in furious guise,
  Along the Appian way.

He made a feast, drank fierce and fast,
  And crown'd his hair with flowers—
No easier nor no quicker pass'd
  The impracticable hours.

The brooding East with awe beheld
  Her impious younger world.
The Roman tempest swell'd and swell'd,
  And on her head was hurled.

The East bow'd low before the blast
  In patient, deep disdain;
She let the legions thunder past,
  And plunged in thought again.

MATTHEW ARNOLD.

GENSERIC

Genseric, King of the Vandals, who, having
    laid waste seven lands,
From Tripolis far as Tangier, from the sea to
    the great desert sands,
Was lord of the Moor and the African,—thirst-
    ing anon for new slaughter,
Sail'd out of Carthage, and sail'd o'er the
    Mediterranean water;
Plunder'd Palermo, seiz'd Sicily, sack'd the
    Lucanian coast,
And paused, and said, laughing, "Where next?"
        Then there came to the Vandal a Ghost
From the Shadowy Land that lies hid and
    unknown in the Darkness Below.
And answered, "To Rome!"
        Said the King to the Ghost, "And
            whose envoy art thou?

Whence com'st thou? and name me his name
    that hath sent thee: and say what is
    thine."
"From far: and His name that hath sent me
    is God," the Ghost answered, "and mine
Was Hannibal once, ere thou wast: and the
    name that I now have is Fate.
But arise, and be swift, and return. For
    God waits, and the moment is late."
And, "I go," said the Vandal. And went.
    When at last to the gates he was come,
Loud he knock'd with his fierce iron fist. And
    full drowsily answer'd him Rome.
"Who is it that knocketh so loud? Get thee
    hence. Let me be. For 'tis late."
"Thou art wanted," cried Genseric. "Open!
    His name that hath sent me is Fate,
And mine, who knock late, Retribution."
            Rome gave him her glorious things;
The keys she had conquer'd from kingdoms:
    the crowns she had wrested from kings:
And Genseric bore them away into Carthage,
    avenged thus on Rome,
And paused, and said, laughing, "Where next?"
            And again the Ghost answer'd him,
            "Home!

For now God doth need thee no longer."
        "Where leadest thou me by the
            hand?"
Cried the King to the Ghost. And the Ghost
answer'd, "Into the Shadowy Land."
                        OWEN MEREDITH.

KUBLA KHAN

In Xanadu did Kubla Khan
    A stately pleasure-dome decree:
Where Alph, the sacred river, ran
Through caverns measureless to man
    Down to a sunless sea.
So twice five miles of fertile ground
With walls and towers were girdled round:
And there were gardens bright with sinuous rills
Where blossom'd many an incense-bearing tree;
And here were forests ancient as the hills,
Enfolding sunny spots of greenery.
But O, that deep romantic chasm which slanted
Down the green hill athwart a cedarn cover!
A savage place! as holy and enchanted
As e'er beneath a waning moon was haunted
By woman wailing for her demon-lover!
And from this chasm, with ceaseless turmoil
    seething,

As if this earth in fast thick pants were breath-
    ing,
A mighty fountain momently was forced;
Amid whose swift half-intermitted burst
Huge fragments vaulted like rebounding hail,
Or chaffy grain beneath the thresher's flail:
And 'mid these dancing rocks at once and ever
It flung up momently the sacred river.
Five miles meandering with a mazy motion
Through wood and dale the sacred river ran,
Then reached the caverns measureless to man,
And sank in tumult to a lifeless ocean:
And 'mid this tumult Kubla heard from far
Ancestral voices prophesying war!
    The shadow of the dome of pleasure
        Floated midway on the waves;
    Where was heard the mingled measure
        From the fountain and the caves.
It was a miracle of rare device,
A sunny pleasure-dome with caves of ice!

    A damsel with a dulcimer
        In a vision once I saw:
    It was an Abyssinian maid,
        And on her dulcimer she play'd,
    Singing of Mount Abora.

Could I revive within me
  Her symphony and song,
To such a deep delight 'twould win me
That with music loud and long,
I would build that dome in air,
That sunny dome! those caves of ice!
And all who heard should see them there,
And all should cry, Beware! Beware!
His flashing eyes, his floating hair!
Weave a circle round him thrice,
  And close your eyes with holy dread,
  For he on honey-dew hath fed,
And drunk the milk of Paradise.

SAMUEL TAYLOR COLERIDGE.

SOMETHING TO REMEMBER

Ah, did you once see Shelley plain,
  And did he stop and speak to you,
And did you speak to him again?
  How strange it seems, and new!

But you were living before that.
  And also you are living after,
And the memory I started at—
  My starting moves your laughter!

I crossed a moor, with a name of its own
  And a certain use in the world, no-doubt,
Yet a hand's-breadth of it shines alone
  'Mid the blank miles round about:

For there I picked up on the heather
  And there I put inside my breast
A moulted feather, an eagle-feather!
  Well, I forget the rest.

ROBERT BROWNING.

RING OUT, WILD BELLS

Ring out, wild bells, to the wild sky,
    The flying cloud, the frosty light:
    The year is dying in the night;
Ring out wild bells, and let him die.

Ring out the old, ring in the new,
    Ring, happy bells, across the snow:
    The year is going, let him go;
Ring out the false, ring in the true.

Ring out the grief that saps the mind,
    For those that here we see no more;
    Ring out the feud of rich and poor.
Ring in redress to all mankind.

Ring out a slowly dying cause,
    And ancient forms of party strife;
    Ring in the nobler modes of life,
With sweeter manners, purer laws.

Ring out the want, the care, the sin,
    The faithless coldness of the times;
    Ring out, ring out my mournful rhymes,
But ring the fuller minstrel in.

Ring out false pride in place and blood,
    The civic slander and the spite;
    Ring in the love of truth and right,
Ring in the common love of good.

Ring out old shapes of foul disease;
    Ring out the narrowing lust of gold;
    Ring out the thousand wars of old,
Ring in the thousand years of peace.

Ring in the valiant man and free,
    The larger heart, the kindlier hand;
    Ring out the darkness of the land,
Ring in the Christ that is to be.

                    ALFRED, LORD TENNYSON.

INDEX OF AUTHORS

INDEX OF FIRST LINES

CAMBRIDGE: PRINTED BY JOHN CLAY, M.A. AT THE UNIVERSITY PRESS.

Books on
English Language and Literature
published by the
Cambridge University Press

ENGLISH LANGUAGE

English Grammar: Descriptive and Historical. By T. G. TUCKER, Litt D., and R S. WALLACE, M.A. Crown 8vo. 3*s*. net.

A Junior Graphic Grammar. By E. A. A. VARNISH and J. H. HANLY. Crown 8vo. With a table. 2*s*. net.

The Elements of English Grammar. With a Chapter on Essay-writing. By A. S. WEST, M.A. Extra fcap. 8vo. 3*s*. net.

A Chapter on **Essay-writing**, separately. 6*d*. net.

An English Grammar for Beginners. By A. S. WEST, M.A. Extra fcap. 8vo 150th to 175th Thousand. 1*s*. 3*d*. net.

The Revised English Grammar. A new edition of **The Elements of English Grammar,** based upon the recommendations of the Committee on Grammatical Terminology. By A. S. WEST, M.A. Extra fcap. 8vo. 3*s*. net.

The Revised English Grammar for Beginners. A new edition of **English Grammar for Beginners.** By A. S. WEST, M.A. Extra fcap. 8vo. 1*s*. 3*d*. net.

Key to the Questions contained in West's *Revised English Grammar* and *Revised English Grammar for Beginners.* By A. S. WEST, M.A. Extra fcap. 8vo. 4*s*. net. Suitable for use with both the original and revised editions.

A Handbook of English for Junior and Intermediate Classes. By D. B. NICOLSON, M.A. Crown 8vo. 1*s*. 9*d*. net.

English Composition: with Chapters on Précis Writing, Prosody, and Style. By W MURISON, M A. Crown 8vo. 5*s* net. Or in two parts, 3*s*. net each.

Key to the Exercises in *English Composition.* By W. MURISON, M A. Crown 8vo. 5*s* net.

Précis-Writing. By W. MURISON Crown 8vo. In three parts Part I, 3*s*. net. Part II. 3*s*. 6*d*. net. Part III, 4*s*. net.

A Handbook of Précis-Writing. With graduated exercises. By E. D. EVANS, M.A. Crown 8vo. 2*s* 6*d*. net.

An Elementary Old English Grammar (Early West-Saxon). By A J. WYATT, M.A Crown 8vo. 5*s*. net.

An Elementary Old English Reader (Early West-Saxon). By the same author. Crown 8vo. 5*s*. net.

A Concise Anglo-Saxon Dictionary for the use of Students. By JOHN R. CLARK HALL. Second Edition. Revised and enlarged. Demy 8vo. 15s. net.

The Pronunciation of English. Phonetics and Phonetic Transcriptions. By DANIEL JONES, M.A. Crown 8vo. 3s. net. (Cambridge Primers of Pronunciation.)
Wall-charts for class use:
1. The Organs of Speech. On card 2s. 6d. net, on paper 2s net. Mounted on canvas, varnished, with rollers, 3s. 6d. net, mounted on canvas, folded, 4s. 6d. net.
2. English Speech Sounds. On card 2s. 6d. net, on paper 2s. net. Mounted on canvas, varnished, with rollers, 3s. 6d. net; mounted on canvas, folded, 4s. 6d. net.

The Pronunciation of English in Scotland. By WILLIAM GRANT, M.A. Crown 8vo. 4s. net. (Cambridge Primers of Pronunciation.)

Outlines of the History of the English Language. By Professor T. N. TOLLER, M A. Crown 8vo. 4s. 6d. net.

Chapters on English Metre. By JOSEPH B. MAYOR, M.A. Second Edition. Demy 8vo. 7s. 6d. net.

A Handbook of Modern English Metre. By the same author. Extra fcap. 8vo. 2s. 6d. net.

ENGLISH LITERATURE

Beowulf, with the Finnsburg Fragment. Edited by A. J. WYATT. New edition, revised, with introduction and notes, by R. W. CHAMBERS. Demy 8vo. With 2 facsimiles of MSS. 9s. net.

Beowulf. A metrical translation into Modern English. By JOHN R. CLARK HALL. Crown 8vo. 2s. 6d. net.

Spindrift. Salt from the Ocean of English Prose. Edited by GEOFFREY CALLENDER, M.A. Crown 8vo. 3s. 6d. net

Stories from Chaucer. Retold from the Canterbury Tales. With Introduction and Notes by MARGARET C. MACAULAY. Crown 8vo. With frontispiece and 28 illustrations from old MSS. 1s. 9d. net. Without Introduction and Notes. 1s. 3d. net.

The Elder Brother. A Comedy by JOHN FLETCHER. First printed in 1637, now reprinted with slight alterations and abridgement for use on occasions of entertainment, especially in Schools and Colleges. Edited by W. H. DRAPER, M.A. Crown 8vo. With 2 illustrations. 3s. net.

Lyrical Forms in English. Edited with Introduction and Notes by NORMAN HEPPLE, M. Litt. Second Edition Crown 8vo. 2s. 6d. net.

Principles and Method in the Study of English Literature. By W. MACPHERSON, M.A. Crown 8vo. 2s. 6d net.

Milton. Paradise Lost. Edited by A. W. VERITY, M.A. Crown 8vo. 8s. 6d net.

Books on English Language and Literature

Milton. The Poetical Works, edited with Critical Notes by WILLIAM ALDIS WRIGHT, M.A., Litt.D. Crown 8vo. Cloth, 6s. net. India paper, limp lamb-skin, 8s. 6d. net.

On the Art of Writing. Lectures delivered in the University of Cambridge 1913–1914. By Sir ARTHUR QUILLER-COUCH, M.A. Demy 8vo. 7s. 6d. net.

Tennyson. In Memoriam. Edited with a Commentary by ARTHUR W. ROBINSON, B.D. Crown 8vo. 3s. net.

The Literature of the Victorian Era. By Professor HUGH WALKER, LL.D. Crown 8vo. 10s. 6d. net.

Outlines of Victorian Literature. By HUGH WALKER, LL.D., and Mrs HUGH WALKER. Demy 8vo. 3s. 6d. net.

A Book of Victorian Poetry and Prose. Compiled by Mrs HUGH WALKER. Crown 8vo. 3s. 6d. net.

Jonathan Swift. The Leslie Stephen Lecture delivered before the University of Cambridge on 26 May, 1917. By CHARLES WHIBLEY, M.A. Crown 8vo. 1s. 6d. net.

A Primer of English Literature. By W. T. YOUNG, M.A. Small crown 8vo. Cloth, gilt lettering. 2s. 3d. net. School edition. Limp cloth. 1s. 3d. net.

CAMBRIDGE ANTHOLOGIES

Life in Shakespeare's England. A Book of Elizabethan Prose compiled by J. D. WILSON, M.A. Illustrated. 4s. net.

An Anthology of the Poetry of the Age of Shakespeare. Chosen by W. T. YOUNG, M.A. Crown 8vo. 3s. net.

ENGLISH ROMANTIC POETS

Selections from the Poems of John Keats. Edited by A. HAMILTON THOMPSON, M.A., F.S.A. Crown 8vo. 2s. net.

Selections from the Poems of Percy Bysshe Shelley. Edited by A. H. THOMPSON. Crown 8vo. 2s. net.

Selections from the Poems of Samuel Taylor Coleridge. Edited by A H. THOMPSON. Crown 8vo. 2s. net.

PITT PRESS SERIES, ETC.

Bacon's Essays. Edited by A. S. WEST, M.A. 3s. net.

Bacon's History of the Reign of King Henry VII. Edited by the Rev. J. R. LUMBY, D.D 3s. 6d. net

Bacon. New Atlantis. Edited by G. C. MOORE SMITH, M.A 2s net.

Ballads and Poems Illustrating English History. Edited by FRANK SIDGWICK. 2s. net.
Without introduction and notes 1s. 6d. net.

Old Ballads. Edited by FRANK SIDGWICK. 2s. net.

Robert Browning. A Selection of Poems (1835–1864). Edited by W T. YOUNG, M.A. 3s. net.

Burke. Reflections on the French Revolution. Edited by W. ALISON PHILLIPS, M.A., and CATHERINE BEATRICE PHILLIPS. 4s. 6d. net.

ι   ꝺ

Burke. **Speeches on American Taxation and** Conciliation with America. Edited by A. D. INNES, M.A. 3s. 6d. net. Speech on Conciliation with America, separately. 2s. net.

Burke. **Thoughts on the Cause of the Present** Discontents. Edited by W. MURISON, M.A. 3s. net.

Byron. **Childe Harold's Pilgrimage.** Edited by A. H. THOMPSON, M.A. 3s. net.

Chaucer. **The Prologue and The Knight's Tale.** Edited by M. BENTINCK SMITH, M.A. 3s. net

Chaucer. **The Clerkes Tale and The Squieres** Tale. Edited by L. WINSTANLEY, M.A 3s. net.

Chaucer. **The Nonnë Prestes Tale.** Edited by L. WINSTANLEY, M.A. 2s. 3d. net.

Cowley's Prose Works. Edited by J. R. LUMBY. 4s. 6d. net.

De Foe. **Robinson Crusoe.** Part I. Edited by J. HOWARD B MASTERMAN, M.A. 2s. 6d. net.

Earle. **Microcosmography.** Edited by A. S. WEST, M.A. 3s. 6d. net.

Goldsmith. **The Traveller and the Deserted** Village. Edited by W. MURISON, M.A. 1s. 9d. net.

Gray. **English Poems.** Edited by D. C. TOVEY, M.A. 4s. 6d. net.

Extracts from the above
Ode on the Spring and the Bard. 1s. net.
Ode on the Spring and Elegy in a Country Churchyard. 1s. net.

Gray's English Poems. Edited by R. F. CHARLES, M.A. 2s. 3d. net.

Kingsley. **The Heroes, or Greek Fairy Tales for** my Children. Edited with Notes, Illustrations from Greek Vases, and Two Maps, by ERNEST GARDNER, M.A. 1s. 9d. net. Without introduction and notes. 1s. 3d. net.

Lamb's Essays of Elia and Last Essays of Elia. Edited by A. H. THOMPSON, M.A 3s net each.

Lamb, Charles and Mary. **A Selection of Tales** from Shakespeare. With Introduction and Notes, and an Appendix of Extracts from Shakespeare, by J. H. FLATHER, M.A. 1s. 9d. net. A second selection. By the same editor. 1s 9d. net.

Macaulay. **The Lays of Ancient Rome, and other** Poems. Edited by J. H. FLATHER, M.A. 1s. 6d. net.

Macaulay. **John Milton.** Edited, with Introduction and Notes, by J. H. FLATHER, M.A. 1s. 6d. net.

Macaulay. **History of England, Chapters I—III.** Edited by W. F. REDDAWAY, M.A. 2s. 6d. net.

Macaulay. Lord Clive. Edited by A. D. INNES, M.A. 2*s.* net.

By the same editor

Warren Hastings. 2*s.* net.

Two Essays on William Pitt, Earl of Chatham. 3*s.* net.

Essay on The Pilgrim's Progress. 1*s.* 6*d.* net.

Nineteenth Century Essays. Edited with Introduction and Notes by GEORGE SAMPSON. 2*s.* 3*d.* net.

THE CAMBRIDGE MILTON FOR SCHOOLS

With Introduction, Notes and Glossaries, by
A. W. VERITY, M.A.

Arcades. 2*s.* net. **Samson Agonistes.** 3*s.* net.

Ode on the Morning of Christ's Nativity, L'Allegro, Il Penseroso, and Lycidas. 3*s.* net. **Sonnets.** 2*s.* net.

Comus and Lycidas. 2*s.* 6*d.* net. **Comus,** separately. 1*s.* 6*d.* net.

Paradise Lost. In 6 volumes, each containing 2 books, 2*s.* 3*d* net per volume. (For *Paradise Lost* in one volume see p. 2)

More's Utopia. Edited by J. R. LUMBY, D.D 2*s.* 3*d.* net.

More's History of King Richard III. Edited by J. R. LUMBY, D.D. 4*s.* net.

Pope's Essay on Criticism. Edited by A. S. WEST, M A. 2*s.* 6*d.* net.

Pope's Essay on Man. Edited by A. H. THOMPSON, M.A. 2*s.* 6*d* net.

SCHOOL EDITIONS OF SCOTT'S WORKS

Each volume contains Introduction, Notes and Glossary

Marmion. Edited by J. H. B. MASTERMAN, M.A. 3*s.* net.

The Lady of the Lake. Same editor. 3*s* net.

The Lord of the Isles. Edited by J. H. FLATHER, M.A. 2*s.* 3*d.* net.

The Lay of the Last Minstrel. Same editor. 2*s.* 3*d.* net

A Legend of Montrose. Edited by H. F. M. SIMPSON, M.A. 2*s.* 3*d.* net.

Old Mortality. Edited by J. A. NICKLIN. 2*s.* 3*d.* net.

Kenilworth. Edited by J. H. FLATHER, M.A. 2*s.* 3*d.* net

Quentin Durward. Edited by W. MURISON, M.A. 2*s.* 3*d.* net.

The Talisman. Edited by A. S. GAYE, B A. 2*s.* 3*d.* net.

Woodstock. Same editor. 2*s.* 3*d.* net.

Ingram Content Group UK Ltd.
Milton Keynes UK
UKHW020031040523
421194UK00005B/68